Surgeon Grow

AMERICANS IN REVOLUTIONARY RUSSIA

Vol. 1
Albert Rhys Williams, *Through the Russian Revolution*, edited by
William Benton Whisenhunt (2016)

Vol. 2
Princess Julia Cantacuzène, Countess Spéransky, née Grant, *Russian People: Revolutionary Recollections*, edited by Norman E. Saul (2016)

Vol. 3
Ernest Poole, *The Village: Russian Impressions*, edited by Norman E. Saul (2017)

Vol. 4
John Reed, *Ten Days That Shook the World*, edited by
William Benton Whisenhunt (2017)

Vol. 5
Louise Bryant, *Six Red Months in Russia*, edited by Lee A. Farrow (2017)

Vol. 6
Edward Alsworth Ross, *Russia in Upheaval*, edited by Rex A. Wade (2017)

Vol. 7
Donald Thompson, *Donald Thompson in Russia*, edited by David H. Mould (2017)

Vol. 8
Arthur Bullard, *The Russian Pendulum: Autocracy—Democracy—Bolshevism*, edited by
David W. McFadden (2019)

Vol. 9
David Francis, *Russia from the American Embassy*, edited by Vladimir V. Noskov (2019)

Vol. 10
Pauline S. Crosley, *Intimate Letters from Petrograd*, edited by Lee A. Farrow (2019)

Vol. 11
Madeleine Z. Doty, *"The Bolshevik Revolution Had Descended on Me": Madeleine Z. Doty's Russian Revolution*, edited by Julia L. Mickenberg (2019)

Vol. 12
John R. Mott, the American YMCA, and Revolutionary Russia, edited by Matthew Lee Miller (2020)

Vol. 13
Carl W. Ackerman, *Trailing the Bolsheviki: Twelve Thousand Miles with the Allies in Siberia*, edited by Ivan Kurilla (2020)

Vol. 14
Charles Edward Russell, *Unchained Russia*, edited by Rex A. Wade (2021)

Vol. 15
James L. Houghteling, Jr., *A Diary of the Russian Revolution*, edited by David S. Foglesong (2022)

Vol. 16
Malcolm C. Grow, *Surgeon Grow: An American in the Russian Fighting*, edited by Laurie S. Stoff (2022)

Series General Editors:
Norman E. Saul and William Benton Whisenhunt

Surgeon Grow

An American in the Russian Fighting

Malcolm C. Grow

Edited and Introduction by
Laurie S. Stoff

ANTHEM PRESS

Anthem Press
An imprint of Wimbledon Publishing Company
www.anthempress.com

First published by Slavica Publishers, Indiana University, USA, 2022

This edition first published in UK and USA 2026
by ANTHEM PRESS
75–76 Blackfriars Road, London SE1 8HA, UK
or PO Box 9779, London SW19 7ZG, UK
and
244 Madison Ave #116, New York, NY 10016, USA

Copyright © 2026 Laurie S. Stoff editorial matter and selection;
individual chapters © individual contributors

The moral right of the authors has been asserted.

All rights reserved. Without limiting the rights under copyright reserved above,
no part of this publication may be reproduced, stored or introduced into
a retrieval system, or transmitted, in any form or by any means
(electronic, mechanical, photocopying, recording or otherwise),
without the prior written permission of both the copyright
owner and the above publisher of this book.

British Library Cataloguing-in-Publication Data
A catalogue record for this book is available from the British Library.

Library of Congress Cataloging-in-Publication Data
A catalog record for this book has been requested.

ISBN-13: 978-1-83999-732-7 (Hbk)
ISBN-10: 1-83999-732-X (Hbk)

ISBN-13: 978-1-83999-733-4 (Pbk)
ISBN-10: 1-83999-733-8 (Pbk)

Cover design: Tracey Theriault

This title is also available as an eBook.

CONTENTS

Editor's Introduction   ix
   Laurie S. Stoff

SURGEON GROW:
AN AMERICAN IN THE RUSSIAN FIGHTING

Foreword	5
I. I Go to Russia	9
II. Two Weeks of Sight-Seeing	14
III. The Hussars Hospital at Tsarskoe-Selo	18
IV. Preparing To Go to the Front	23
V. Off to the Front	27
VI. The Spectacle in the Frozen Lake	33
VII. The Professor of Mathematics	38
VIII. In the Russian Trenches	43

IX. I Go "Over the Top"		52
X. I Meet the Czar		63
XI. Over the German Lines		70
XII. Through a Shower of Shells		74
XIII. The Battle of Postovy		80
XIV. The Dogs of War		86
XV. Sound Sleepers		89
XVI. Injured by a Shell		93
XVII. The Medal of St. George		97
XVIII. A Demonstration Attack		100
XIX. We Join Brusiloff's Big Drive		108
XX. The Battle of the Stockhod		118
XXI. We Break Through!		126
XXII. A Blind Army		131
XXIII. The Gas Attack		135
XXIV. The Revolution		137
XXV. After the Revolution		143
Index		149

EDITOR'S INTRODUCTION
Laurie S. Stoff

Malcolm Cummings Grow was born on November 19, 1887, in Philadelphia. He received his medical degree from Jefferson Medical College in 1909, having specialized in internal medicine. When the First World War began, he was in private practice in his home city. In August 1915, he visited Washington, DC, where he became acquainted with Dr. Edward Egbert, who at the time was serving as chief surgeon of the American Red Cross Hospital in Kiev and was on a brief leave. Egbert described the dire situation concerning Russia's military medical services, particularly its shortage of qualified doctors, and persuaded Grow to offer his expertise to the war effort there. Grow was sympathetic to the Russian plight while also eager for the opportunity to further develop his surgical skills, and was lured by the excitement of war. As a result, he agreed to accompany Egbert back to Russia. One month later, he arrived in the Russian capital, Petrograd.[1]

Initially, Grow served as a civilian doctor at one of the medical facilities (which he called the "Hussar Hospital")[2] located at Tsarskoe Selo, a small suburban village outside of Petrograd where one of the imperial palaces (Tsar Nicholas II's preferred residence) was located. Working safely behind the lines was not what he had in mind, and therefore he began pursuing the opportunity of joining the Russian military at the front. He was introduced to Colonel Andrei Ivanovich Kalpashnikov-Camac (Kalpaschnecoff in Grow's writing), a noble scion from a prominent Penza family. Kalpashnikov's connections in both American and Russian society undoubtedly made him a logical choice to help Grow achieve his goal. His mother was a godchild

---

[1] The original name of the city, St. Petersburg, was changed when the war broke out because it sounded too "German."

[2] Most likely, Grow was referring to the infirmary of the Life (Imperial) Guards of the Hussar Regiment. There were more than eighty other medical facilities established at Tsarskoe Selo and in neighboring Pavlosk during the war. The Empress Aleksandra Feodorovna, who trained as a nurse along with her two eldest daughters, Olga and Tat'iana, organized Hospital No. 3 in the palace itself. There was a separate officers' wing organized in one of the outbuildings of the Palace Hospital. There were also medical facilities established in the Charitable Home for Disabled Warriors, the Officers' Artillery School, the Serafim Refugee Shelter No. 79, the Cathedral of St. Fedorov, the Holy Trinity Sister of Mercy Community, and the private homes of S. P. Shuvanov, E. G. Volters, and the Kokorev mansion.

of Tsar Alexander II and descended from Peter the Great's mother, while his father's sister married Philadelphia notable John Burgess Camac, with whom Kalpashnikov lived in Paris until the age of 12 (after which Camac was officially added to his family name). After attending law school in Russia, he was sent to Washington as an attaché to the Russian embassy. In 1913, he was transferred back to Petrograd to serve in the foreign office. When war broke out, although exempt from military service as a result of his diplomatic status, Kalpashnikov volunteered for service in the Russian Red Cross. Despite the fact that he had no medical training, he was assigned as commander of the 21st Flying Column, attached to the 1st Siberian Army Corps.[3] Grow convinced the colonel that he could be of more use at the front, and as a result of Kalpashnikov's efforts, he received a military appointment—commissioned as a lieutenant colonel in the Imperial Russian Medical Corps.

Grow possessed no military experience and spoke very little Russian, but nonetheless was able to secure a fairly high rank in the Russian Imperial Army Medical Corps as well as a position in a frontline medical unit, largely as the result of his acquaintance with the "right" people. He related how Colonel Kalpashnikov was able to cut through the notoriously heavy bureaucracy of the Russian Red Cross, barraging his way through the offices of the administration, brushing aside secretaries like flies until he had the ears of the top brass, who readily complied with his request to commission Grow and dispatch with Kalpashnikov's flying column to replace the surgeon he had just lost in the field. The shortage of qualified surgeons in Russia undoubtedly made this a more compelling case. Grow served as regimental surgeon under Kalpashnikov on the Russian Western Front, where the army was engaged against the Germans, and then was transferred with the unit to the Southwestern

---

[3] During and after the war, Kalpashnikov continued his American connections. In 1916, he led a successful mission to the US to raise funds for the purchase of American ambulances for the Russian Red Cross. In September 1917, he went to Jassy (Iasi), Romania, to serve as a representative of the Russian Red Cross at the headquarters of the American Red Cross, and remained there until just after the October Revolution, when he returned to Petrograd. He was arrested in late December 1917 and held for several months on false charges of taking American money to fund opposition to the Bolsheviks and tsarist sympathies. He made a failed attempt to escape his prison cell in the Peter and Paul Fortress, and was only saved from being shot by the fact that the Bolshevik government was in turmoil in the process of moving to Moscow. After being interrogated by Felix Dzerzhinsky, head of the Cheka (secret police), he was released at the end of April 1918. After narrowly escaping rearrest, he fled Russia with false papers and moved to the United States. See George F. Kennan, *Soviet-American Relations, 1917–1920, Vol. 1: Russia Leaves the War* (Princeton, NJ: Princeton University Press, 1956), 191–218; and Andrew Kalpaschnikoff [sic], *A Prisoner of Trotsky's* (New York: Doubleday, Page, 1920). For more on the American Ambulance, see Joshua Segal, "American Humanitarian Volunteerism in Russia's Military 1914–1917" (PhD diss., George Washington University, 2018).

Front to fight the Austro-Hungarians in the massive offensive that took place in the spring of 1916.

Grow left Russia and went back to the United States briefly in 1916 on leave, and then again in January 1917 in an attempt to secure supplies and vehicles to transport wounded soldiers for Russia's medical services. He was held up in Christiana, Denmark, however, as a result of a German blockade, and was forced to remain there until March. As a result, he was not in the country when the February Revolution that brought down the tsarist regime occurred; rather, he received news of it while awaiting permission to depart for the US. In July 1917, he returned to Russia, serving as part of an American Red Cross mission in Vladivostok. He was anxious to be reunited with his old unit at the front, and did so in August for a week. Distraught by what he witnessed there, he went back to Petrograd, but left Russia for the US before the October Revolution.

Back in the United States, Grow joined the US Army Medical Services. After a number of years of service, he achieved the rank of general. In 1934, he was appointed the chief flight surgeon of the Army Air Corps, a position in which he served until 1939. Along with Major General Harry Armstrong, he established the Aero Medical Laboratory at Wright-Patterson Air Force Base in Ohio. While working there, Grow was instrumental in the development of light body armor and steel helmets to protect air combat crews from wounds incurred by low-velocity missiles. The work he did in this area yielded him the Legion of Merit. He also earned the Distinguished Service Medal for his role in creating a number of innovative items used to protect combat personnel from a variety of hazards. He also established a new system of rest homes, a special pass system, and training for medical officers in tactical unit.

In 1945, Grow was appointed acting air surgeon for the Army Air Forces and air surgeon in 1946. He then became the first surgeon general for the US Air Force in 1949, and served in that role until November of that year. Grow retired from the Air Force in December 1949 and passed away in October 1960. The Malcolm Grow Medical Center at Andrews Air Force Base is named in his honor.

Grow's Experiences on the Russian Front

Dr. Grow arrived in Russia after the country had already been fighting a total war for an entire year and was struggling considerably against its adversaries. From the very start of the conflict, Russia experienced serious problems with the production and distribution of supply and support service, resulting in shortages of weapons, ammunition, artillery, food, and other materials necessary to wage mechanized warfare. The tsarist administration and military establishment were both weighed down by inefficiency and corruption. Additionally, poor leadership and strategic planning plagued nearly all levels of the military and the industrial systems that were supposed to support it. The result was a nation struggling considerably against the better-trained and equipped Germans. The Russian Imperial Army had suffered significant defeats at the hands of the Germans in a number of battles during the first year of the war. Particularly devasting blows came at Tannenburg and the Masurian Lakes in the fall of 1914. Greater success was achieved against the Austro-Hungarian Army in Galicia and Bukhovina. But the Central Powers launched a massive offensive in April 1915, the result of which was a sustained retreat by the Russian Army for the next five months, during which Russian forces were pushed back hundreds of miles. Thus, when Grow finally arrived at the front, although it had finally stopped retreating, the army was stinging from its significant losses: casualties of over one million, another million captured, and the loss of extensive territory in Poland, Lithuania, and Belorussia.[4]

Indeed, Russia struggled throughout the war to provide its military with adequate medical care. Upon the outbreak of hostilities in August 1914, the Russian government began mobilizing resources and personnel for the war effort. However, similar problems of production and distribution of goods and obstacles in organization and provision of services affected medical work. Russian officials were caught somewhat off guard by the scope of total war (despite warnings from those who had experienced these difficulties in the Russo-Japanese War) and had not correctly anticipated the vast numbers of medical personnel, facilities, equipment, and supplies that would be required. The extensive scale of the war coupled with the lack of experience and reluctance to utilize civilian sources of support often hindered efficient provision of medical services.[5] This would prove troublesome for the Russian Armed Forces, which suffered particularly high casualties: by September 1917, the numbers of Russian troops wounded in the war was approximately 2.5 million, and another 2.3 million soldiers had fallen ill as a result of the spread of highly contagious epidemic diseases (typhoid fever, typhus, cholera, and dysentery, as well as other illness such as pneumonia or scurvy).[6] For many (both the soldiers who contracted them and the medical personnel who treated them), these illnesses proved fatal.[7] Ultimately, this caused a breakdown in public health and contributed to an already shaky confidence in the tsarist system to meet the needs of its people.

---

[4] On the military aspects of Russia's Great War, see Norman Stone, *The Eastern Front, 1914–1917* (New York: Scribners, 1975); David R. Stone, *The Russian Army in the Great War: The Eastern Front, 1914–1917* (Lawrence: University Press of Kansas, 2015); and Joshua Sanborn, *Imperial Apocalypse: The Great War and the Destruction of the Russian Empire* (New York: Oxford University Press, 2015).

[5] John F. Hutchinson, *Politics and Public Health in Revolutionary Russia, 1890–1918* (Baltimore: Johns Hopkins University Press, 1990), 110.

[6] Tsentral'noe Statisticheskoe Upravlenie, Otdel Voennoi Statistiki, *Rossiia v mirovoi voine, 1914–1918 goda (v tsifrakh)* (Moscow: Tipografia M. K. Kh. imeni F. Ia. Lavrova, 1925), 25.

[7] Ibid., 99.

Because the Russian military medical corps was significantly underprepared for the treatment of the millions of ill and wounded soldiers that soon flooded in, it quickly became reliant on a number of civilian organizations to supplement care. These included the Russian Red Cross Society and a number of voluntary organs associated with the Union of Zemstvos and the Union of Towns (collectively known as Zemgor), which played vital roles in the provision of wartime services. Zemgor organs were an amalgam of local efforts, charged with medical, sanitary, and food provisioning duties for both the military and civilian populations.[8] They were staffed by some professionals, but many more volunteers, including thousands of women, who received very quick and cursory training before being put to work.

Despite the good intentions and positive actions of these groups, as well as the intense need for their services, the autocracy as well as the military establishment remained wary of them (and most civil society efforts) and their staffs of liberal professionals, many of whom opposed the tsarist system. In an attempt to maintain centralized control over wartime medical services, the Russian Red Cross Society, the most trusted of these organizations (although not immune to problematic relationships with government and military authorities), was assigned sole responsibility over the front and given exclusive authority to operate across the line of demarcation that was supposed to separate the active war zone from the rear.[9] All other organizations providing medical services were limited to evacuating soldiers away from the front and treating them in the rear. The central government's original desire was to cut off the rest of the country from the regions directly affected by the war. The Union of Zemstvos and the Union of Towns thus were placed under the "flag" of the Red Cross, in a subordinate position to the latter, and in the rear only. These organizations and their personnel suffered from conflicts with the central government, the Red Cross, and with one another. Even the Russian Imperial Army, despite its dependence on such aid, expressed resistance, and was somewhat hostile to interference from civilian quarters. The Russian Red Cross in particular had been unable to overcome pre-war accusations of corruption, ineptitude, and acting to curry political favor that had convinced some military medical officials that the Russian Red Cross was a "weak entity" that had "lost its constructive energy," unable to undertake effective action.[10]

---

[8] For more on the Zemgor organizations, see William Gleason, "The All-Russian Union of Towns and the All-Russian Union of Zemstvos in World War I, 1914–1917" (PhD diss., Indiana University, 1972).

[9] The highly mobile nature of the war on the Eastern Front, unlike the more stagnant positional warfare of the Western Front, made this largely impossible and impractical, as frontlines shifted quickly and often.

[10] "Otchet doktora meditsiny S. K. Solov′ev, zaveduiuvaiushchii meditsinkoi chastiu severnom front," Rossiiskii gosudarstvennyi voenno-istoricheskii arkhiv, fond 12674, opis 1, delo 10, listi 374–77 (Report of medical doctor S. K. Solov′ev, supervisor of medical units on the Northern Front, Russian State Military-Historical Archive), hereafter RGVIA.

The overly bureaucratic nature of the Russian Red Cross beleaguered the organization and meant that the smallest actions required permission from some higher authority. Waiting for such approval was often painstakingly long and prevented medical personnel from carrying out important activities when immediately necessary.[11]

Shortages of trained medical personnel, especially doctors, were particularly acute in the Russian military medical corps. Thus, the appeal made by Grow, an experienced surgeon, to join the efforts at the front, was likely welcomed by Russian officials. Nonetheless, assignment to a frontline unit was seen as a turn of good luck. Even Dr. Egbert, who had convinced him to give up the safety and security of his private practice in Philadelphia and join the war effort in Russia, expressed his jealousy at Grow's frontline assignment. Egbert lamented that he was stuck in a rear hospital while Grow was going to where the "real" action was. Such sentiments were fairly common among medical workers in Russia, as many were reluctant to serve in establishments on the home front and wanted to be as close to the fighting as possible. While many were able to fulfill this desire, others had to be content with staying in the cities and towns, since wounded soldiers only received cursory medical treatment at the front before being dispatched to the rear for further treatment, surgery, and recovery.

Despite the seeming wisdom of such a strategy—removing the wounded from areas of continued danger and providing them with extended and more comprehensive care—it was not effectively implemented. At the beginning of the campaign, there were very few frontline units of the Red Cross. Military commanders were often reluctant to send non-military organizations and personnel into the war zone. With insufficient numbers of Red Cross units at or near the front, and with the Red Cross (at least initially) being the only non-military organization allowed in active frontline areas, other groups equipped to offer medical support for the army found themselves unable to extend that aid until they received permission to enter the war zone. This also made it difficult to transport wounded men from the front to medical facilities behind the lines. This problem was complicated by the fact that many of the mobile medical units were only able to perform cursory triage and provide temporary care for wounded and ill soldiers and civilians. According to the medical war plans, this was the sole purpose of such units. Patients who needed further care were to be transported to interior medical facilities, more permanent and extensive establishments in the rear to get further treatment and to recover. This was often impossible, as advances and retreats of troops often cut off these mobile units from roads and railways, forcing them to hold patients much longer and ill-equipped to handle their treatment. Weeks would often go by before the wounded could be evacuated to necessary facilities. Other times, mobile medical units were unable to get to casualties,

---

[11] M. P. Vasilevich, *Polozhenie russkikh plennykh v Germanii i otnoshennie Germanstev k nasileniiu zaniatykh imi oblastei Tsarstva Polskago i Litvy* (Petrograd: A. S. Suvorin "Novoe Vremia," 1917), passim.

who often remained on the battlefields during prolonged attacks. Visiting the front, President of the Russian Duma (parliament) Mikhail Rodzianko was appalled when, at the Warsaw-Vienna railway station, he came across hundreds of wounded men lying on the platform in the rain, receiving little to no medical attention, some with wounds that had remained undressed for five days.[12] Getting the wounded from the battlefields to medical facilities even at the front was extremely challenging. Medical personnel risked their lives extracting the wounded from the battlefields and treating them in frontline dressing stations, as the enemy did not abide by Geneva Convention protocols that prohibited attacks against them and Red Cross facilities.

Serving with a frontline medical unit meant that Grow was "right in the thick of it," witnessing combat up close. This may be why—although he was a surgeon, and his mission with the Russian Army was as a regimental doctor, which ostensibly meant a primary concern with the medical care of wounded and ill soldiers—Grow's narrative focuses much attention on the fighting, particularly his experiences observing operations from the trenches. His work as a doctor is not completely neglected, and there are passages that detail his efforts to serve the wounded, but his story often centers more on the military aspects of his experiences. One might speculate that he thought his readers would be more interested in hearing about the fighting, the close calls with danger, the shelling, his encounters with enemy soldiers, and the political situation in Russia than the medical treatment he was providing. Despite the dangers of serving on the frontlines, Grow seemed to relish these experiences. He was wounded and even temporarily lost his hearing, serving in dressing stations that were extremely close to the fighting and that came under enemy fire. His efforts were rewarded by the Russian imperial government, receiving both the Order of Saint Stanislaus, 3rd class with swords, and the Cross of Saint George, 4th class, for gallantry in action.

Grow's Commentary on Russia and Russians

As an American doctor serving with the Russian army, Grow seemed endlessly fascinated by Russia and its people. He made a number of remarks about Russian culture and customs, often taking time to explain to the reader aspects of Russian daily life, particularly at the front. He seemed to genuinely enjoy the new experiences he had, the food and beverages he tried, the rituals associated with socialization, and other elements of daily life. While he did his best to provide exposition for what he assumed to be an unfamiliar audience, his narrative suffers from some weaknesses and inadequacies. He consistently misspells Russian words, names, and places—usually defaulting to a phonetic interpretation that does not always match closely to the actual verbiage.

---

[12] M. V. Rodzianko, *The Reign of Rasputin: An Empire's Collapse*, trans. Catherine Zvegintzoff (Gulf Breeze, FL: Academic International Press, 1973), 112–16.

Somewhat questionable as well is his repetition of dialogue and conversation by Russians, particularly that of common soldiers and low-ranking medical personnel such as orderlies, who likely spoke no English. Since Grow did not initially speak Russian, we must take his early reports of things said by these individuals either as translations provided by the few officers and other personnel who did know English, or as Grow's interpretations of what was said based on context, body language, and other cues he might have used. As a result, it is likely that at least some of what he reported as speech originating from average Russians was potentially inaccurate. Grow did seem to pick up some Russian language as he served, and eventually, his ability to converse with the average Russian improved. Therefore, his later reportage might be more accurate.

But perhaps more importantly, Grow orientalizes Russia and Russians to a great extent—so even while he applies positive attributes to them, they are still framed as inferior against the standard of the West, and his paternalistic, patronizing attitude pervades much of his commentary. "The Russian is a simple-minded, childlike individual, but he is also an idealist and at heart he loves his fellowmen. Being primitive, his passions, either of love or hate, admiration or scorn, are naturally colossal. He is also sensitive to extraneous influences," he remarked.[13] His comments reflect very common stereotypes and simplified conceptualizations about Russian soldiers: strong, stoic, patriotic, willing to endure great hardships, loyal but simple, even primitive (conceptions held by Westerners about Russian people in general at this time). These are consistent with Russian elite attitudes about peasant-soldiers as well as entirely in line with official pro-war attitudes expressed in patriotic publications. While Grow's work was published in the US and therefore not required to pass the kind of censorship controls that Russian works were subjected to during the war, his commentary is entirely in line with the official rhetoric about the war.

Grow also reflected very common attitudes of the Entente, including the pro-war public in Russia, concerning the Germans and their "barbarity" during the war. He expressed some surprise at the acts of a supposedly "cultured" people, such as bombing and shelling Red Cross facilities, commenting that should they have been "wild savages," such as Africans, he would have not been shocked. These were widespread notions that, from the beginning of the war, were used as propaganda to drum up support for the war.[14] Grow, therefore, is very much a product of the time and place in which he operates.

---

[13] Malcolm C. Grow, *Surgeon Grow: An American in the Russian Fighting* (New York: Frederick A. Stokes, 1918), x–xi.

[14] On wartime propaganda, see Stephen Norris, *A War of Images: Russian Popular Prints, Wartime Culture, and National Identity, 1812–1945* (DeKalb: Northern Illinois University Press, 2006); and Hubertus F. Jahn, *Patriotic Culture in Russia during World War I* (Ithaca, NY: Cornell University Press, 1995).

Somewhat surprisingly, despite the fact that in the provision of medical services in Russia during the war female nurses outnumbered doctors three to one, and many thousands served on the front lines, Grow only mentioned encountering nurses once, and that was during his brief service in the rear. Although official regulations sought to keep them at least three to four miles behind the lines, women were often found in medical units very close to the fighting. Thus, while frontline units like Grow's flying column were supposed to be staffed by male personnel, with medical students and orderlies providing support to doctors, in many cases female nurses ended up comprising the staffs of these units.[15]

Of the nurses he did mention working with in the hospital at Tsarskoe Selo, however, Grow was very adulatory, commenting:

> All the nurses except one were titled women who, at the beginning of the war, had taken the six months' training course required to become a war-sister. They had given up everything else and devoted themselves resolutely to the task in hand.
>
> The exception was a lady who had been a professional nurse for many years, and who acted as assistant in operations and had charge of the operating room ... All of the sisters spoke English perfectly, many of them having received their education in England and all having travelled and spent much time there. This was a great relief to me and in conjunction with the charming friendliness and courtesy with which I was received quickly put me at my ease.[16]

He complimented them on their expert work, which contrasts with some other western observers of Russian medical services in general, and nurses specifically, who were sometimes critical of the lack of advanced knowledge and other deficiencies of the Russian medical system.

---

[15] See, for example, N. Chelakova, "Iz zapisok sestry miloserdii," *Novoe Russkoe Slovo*, June 1969; Florence Farmborough, *With the Armies of the Tsar: A Nurse at the Russian Front in War and Revolution, 1914–1918* (New York: Cooper Square, 2000); Khristina Semina, *Tragediia russkoi armii pervoi velikoi voiny 1914-1918 gg. Zapiski sestry miloserdiia kavkazskogo fronta* (New Mexico: C. D. Semine, 1964); Violetta Thurstan, *Field Hospital and Flying Column: Being the Journal of an English Nursing Sister in Belgium and Russia* (London: G. P. Putnam's Sons, 1915); Lidja Zakharova, *Dnevnik sestry miloserdiia (na peredovykh pozitsiiakh)* (Petrograd: Izdatel'stvo biblioteka "Velikoi Voiny," 1915); among others. For more on nurses during the war in Russia, see Laurie S. Stoff, *Russia's Sisters of Mercy and the Great War: More than Binding Men's Wounds* (Lawrence: University Press of Kansas, 2015).

[16] Grow, *Surgeon Grow*, 21–22.

Grow stated, "The sisters worked like veteran nurses and everything in the operating-room was like clock-work."[17] The nurses in his view were "tireless," "patient," and "gentle." He remarked that "these women, not one of whom before the war had ever done a stroke of disagreeable work or even had to experience anything unpleasant, went about their tasks cheerfully and smiling, always gentle and kind, caring for those peasant soldiers as though they were their very own children."[18] However, he did note that the Russians suffered from hindrances to proper care resulting from deficiencies in supplies, medicine, and equipment.

Aside from these nurses, women are nearly completely absent from other aspects of his narrative. Other than the (very) occasional encounter with a peasant woman or two, Grow's narrative suggests that he operated in an almost exclusively male preserve. He did mention a female doctor who was serving in the Hussar Hospital at Tsarskoe Selo. This seems odd, especially since, according to an article about Colonel Kalpashnikov's flying column, the very unit in which Grow served, there were two nurses among its personnel.[19] Yet Grow never even mentioned them. It seems that he did not serve directly with them, despite their presence in the unit.

The other exception to this near-total absence of women in Grow's book is a photograph of a young female volunteer with a caption describing her actions. Having disguised herself as a man, she entered the 1st Siberian Army Corps and fought alongside her male compatriots until she was discovered after being wounded in a battle near the town of Postovy and treated at Grow's dressing station. However, this woman, nor the thousands of others who served as soldiers in Russia's Great War, never made it into Grow's narrative. Why he believed that she deserved a picture with a short caption, but little exposition, is unknown. Grow also fails to mention the most striking example of female combat participation, the organization of several all-female units by the Provisional Government that took power following the fall of the tsarist government in the summer of 1917.[20] The all-female battalions were media superstars for the short period of their existence, reported on in publications from Petrograd to New York, and mentioned in most of the other foreign observers' accounts of Russia at this time, and thus it is highly unlikely that Grow would not have heard about them. One such unit, the 1st Russian Women's Battalion of Death, was even assigned to fight with the 1st Siberian Army Corps, the very unit to which

---

[17] Ibid., 22.

[18] Ibid., 28.

[19] "Young Hero Tells of Russia's 'Flying Column' of Red Cross," *The Nashua Reporter* (Nashua, IA), January 25, 1917, 5. My thanks to Joshua Segal for directing me to this source.

[20] For more on women soldiers in Russia during the First World War, see Laurie S. Stoff, *They Fought for the Motherland: Russia's Women Soldiers in World War I and the Revolution* (Lawrence: University Press of Kansas, 2006).

Grow's flying column was attached. Therefore, again, it is somewhat puzzling as to why Grow leaves them out of his book.

Revolution

Grow's memoir not only gives us insight into the experiences of a doctor on the Russian front and a participant in the action of the war, but also glimpses of the turbulent events of the revolutions of 1917. Again, we must take care in accepting his observations uncritically, as they reflect many of the misconceptions and stereotypes of the moment. Grow maintained the idea that Russian soldiers were completely loyal and served well, with no thought of not carrying out their duty, until after the February Revolution (despite the fact that he was not even in Russia when it occurred, having left in January and not returning until July). He seemed entirely surprised by the revolution and completely taken aback by what he saw as a sudden transformation of the once formidable, obedient, and long-suffering Russian troops to a chaotic, undisciplined, petulant, unruly mob. Problems and failures of the Russian military are attributed almost exclusively to nefarious foreign—i.e., German—forces working to sabotage Russia's war effort. He attributed all the dissatisfaction, disruption, and lack of morale in the Russian armed forces to German agitation. He thus presented the revolution as simultaneously coming out of nowhere and the product of treacherous forces working to bring it about. He was convinced that prior to the February Revolution, Russian soldiers were completely committed to the war and fought gallantly despite all of the obstacles they faced. Grow seemed not only to accept the idea that the entire empire was behind the war effort, but the Russian social and political order itself, never questioning the extent to which this proved to be the greatest barrier to Russian military success or that the peasant-soldier ever could have questioned either the legitimacy of the tsarist system or the war itself. In fact, as indicated above, he benefited from the network of connections based on status and influence that was characteristic of life under the old regime.

Rather than acknowledging the extent to which wartime failures were the result of internal problems, Grow wrote about how pro-German agents worked to spread rumors that broke down morale. The only faults he attributed to the Russian soldiers were their childlike naiveté and susceptibility to external influences. Blissfully unaware of his own biases, Grow claimed he was just "telling it like it is":

> The book I have written contains no argument. I have tried to tell the simple story of what I saw, to relate my own experiences and impressions in a purely narrative style, leaving the reader to draw his own conclusions. My earnest desire is to bring plainly before the American people the heroic fight these peasant soldiers put up while suffering under most adverse conditions in the

field and while many baneful influences were at work in the rear, undermining the organization of the Russian government and military machine.[21]

None of this should be surprising, as it was a view held by many Americans at the time. In a review of Grow's book in 1918 in *The Outlook*, with the amazingly original and succinct title "A Good Book on Russia," correspondent and adventurer George Kennan[22] wrote that despite the fact that dozens of Americans had written on the state of Russia preceding, during, and following the revolution, most of the information they conveyed was "superficial, inaccurate, and sensational, and some of it is wholly untrustworthy and misleading."[23]

But Grow's book was not among them, according to Kennan, who largely attributed the failure to accurately depict the Russian situation to a lack of previous knowledge of Russian history and culture. Despite the fact that Grow really did not have any such knowledge, Kennan asserts that he had remained there long enough to get an "accurate" picture of the situation. He particularly notes the time that Grow spent embedded with the Russian army, serving directly on the front lines and in the trenches, getting to know the Russian officers and soldiers.

Kennan repeated the oft-made lament that Grow familiarly echoed concerning the Russian army, one reiterated time and again by other outside observers, and even some insiders, that it was a spectacular fighting force, propelled by undaunted dedication on the part of stoic, courageous, and undyingly loyal peasant-soldiers, but was thwarted by poor leadership, impeded by shortages of weapons, equipment, and ammunition that were the result of betrayal by spies and saboteurs, and undermined by pernicious propaganda. Grow reiterated the common conception that soldiers "never had sufficient rifles" and that "many times they had to wait until rifles could be taken from [the] wounded" and given to them as a result of German intrigue and subterfuge.[24] He called the Russian army "a magnificent fighting machine" prior to the revolution, and argued it was the effects of the post-February (dis)order that caused its ultimate collapse. He took the standard, conservative military line asserting that "had the Provisional Government taken a firm stand from the beginning and failed to recognize the soldiers' committees, backing up the generals and officers in their

---

[21] Grow, *Surgeon Grow*, xi–xii.

[22] This Kennan was the older cousin of the more famous diplomat George F. Kennan, who authored the book mentioned in note 3.

[23] George Kennan, "A Good Book on Russia," *The Outlook: With Illustrations*, vol. 119 (1918): 128.

[24] For the actual reasons behind Russia's supply and distribution problems, many of which were largely resolved by the end of 1915, see Lewis Siegelbaum, *The Politics of Industrial Mobilization in Russia, 1914–1917: A Study of the War-Industries Committees* (New York: St. Martin's Press, 1983).

efforts to enforce discipline and retaining the death penalty for insubordination," the Russian army would have been able to maintain coherence and continue being an effective fighting force. Thus, Grow's contribution fits squarely with the contemporary Western and Russian émigré literature that viewed the revolution as an anomaly, a series of calculated machinations by forces working against the interests of Russia.

While his ideas were consistent with commonly-held contemporary views of Russia's dedication to the war effort, and certainly patriotism and nationalism were strong among many in the Russian public during the war,[25] they obscure the numerous internal problems that the Russian armed forces faced, as well as the less-than-enthusiastic attitude of many rank-and-file troops toward the war. Although initial mobilization of troops was largely successful, putting over four million men from disparate areas of the vast empire into battle, there were some problems that revealed underlying tensions. Riots and protests against conscription occurred in several regions.[26] As the war dragged on, but long before the effects of the February Revolution were felt, the Russian army suffered from problems of poor morale and lack of discipline like other armies fighting in this war, including fraternization, voluntary surrender, desertion, insubordination, and war-weariness.[27] All of Grow's commentaries seem oblivious

---

[25] After the war, many scholars, particularly those among the Russian émigré community, advanced the thesis that Russia lacked a well-developed sense of nationalism and national duty, which contributed considerably to its failures in the war. Recently, several historians have argued that a sense of belonging to a national community was strongly present in wartime Russia. See, for example, Melissa Stockdale, *Mobilizing the Russian Nation: Patriotism and Citizenship in the First World War* (Cambridge: Cambridge University Press, 2016). Grow's perceptions support the idea of widespread patriotic support for the war effort, but, at the same time, seem to indicate that some in the West began to doubt this.

[26] Joshua Sanborn, "The Mobilization of 1914 and the Question of the Russian Nation: A Re-Examination," *Slavic Review* 59, no. 2 (2000): 275–77.

[27] For a better understanding of Russian soldiers' attitudes about the war and the breakdown of the army, see Nikolai N. Golovin, *The Russian Army in the World War* (New Haven, CT: Yale University Press, 1931); Joshua Sanborn, *Drafting the Russian Nation: Military Conscription, Total War, and Mass Politics, 1905–1925* (DeKalb: Northern Illinois University Press, 2003); and Allan K. Wildman, *The End of the Russian Imperial Army: The Old Army and the Soldiers' Revolt (March–April, 1917)* (Princeton, NJ: Princeton University Press, 1980) and *The End of the Russian Imperial Army, Volume II: The Road to Soviet Power and Peace* (Princeton, NJ: Princeton University Press, 1987). On more specific problems of the army, see Marc Ferro, "Russia: Fraternization and Revolution," in *Meetings in No Man's Land: Christmas 1914 and Fraternisation in the Great War* (London: Constable, 2007), 212–33; Aleksandr Astashov, "'The Other War' on the Eastern Front during the First World War: Fraternization and Making Peace with the Enemy," in *Military Affairs in Russia's Great War and Revolution, 1914–1922, Book 1: Military Experiences*, ed. Laurie S. Stoff, et al., Russia's Great War & Revolution Series (Bloomington, IN: Slavica, 2019); and Paul Simmons, "Desertion in the Russian Army, 1914–1917," in Stoff, et al., *Military Experiences*. For sources in Russian, see Mikhail S. Frenkin, *Russkaia armiia i revoliutsiia 1917–1918* (Munich: Logos, 1978); A. B. Astashov, "Dezertirstvo i bor′ba s nim v tsarskoi armii v gody

to the manifestations of deeply rooted dissatisfaction with the contemporary social, political, and economic structures and systems, but also the tremendous impact of the total war, which proved to be too great a burden for these systems to endure and thus, in many ways, amplified this discontent and provided opportunities for new political forces to capitalize on imperial failure. He entirely missed that the February Revolution had broad military support as a result of both short and long-term dissatisfaction with the tsarist regime and its incompetency in waging the war. After the February Revolution, which seemed to take him somewhat by surprise, Grow became distraught over what he perceived as licentious behavior on the part of a soldiery that misunderstood the concept of liberty now afforded to them following the fall of tsarism. Instead of accepting the grave responsibility that came with this newfound freedom, the soldiers, according to Grow, merely acted on their base impulses.

Perhaps even more surprising is the nearly complete lack of commentary about the role of the Bolsheviks or any other socialist parties.[28] Grow, unlike Kennan and many other American observers, was uncharacteristically quiet about the spread of socialist ideology among soldiers. In fact, his only mention of any socialist influence came only peripherally, when he claimed that Russian soldiers were in communication with the Industrial Workers of the World (IWW) in late summer 1917. He did not speak about the creation or actions of the Soviets in 1917 or the Bolsheviks in opposing the war and counterrevolution in the unrest during the summer of that year, in their stopping Kornilov's attempted revolt, or in their opposing the Provisional Government. None of the Bolshevik leaders, who were extremely active during the spring and summer of 1917, such as Vladimir Lenin and Lev Trotsky, made it into Grow's story. He did not even connect his numerous reiterations of the effects of German subterfuge to the Bolsheviks, which was an extremely commonly held opinion among many at this time, including the notion that Lenin and the Bolsheviks were German agents. Considering his numerous references to German conspiracies as the source of Russia's troubles, this omission is surprising. Thus, Grow's book stands in stark contrast to many other American accounts of the revolutionary year.

Although such absences are somewhat strange, they might be explained by the fact that Grow's perspective was severely limited. He was no student of Russian history or politics, either before or during his time in the country. He served with a single unit, in specific and delimited areas of the front, and associated primarily with officers and soldiers who seemed fiercely loyal to the tsarist regime. He experienced the war only through these finite and narrow contacts and experiences. Arriving a

---

pervoi mirovoi voiny," *Rossiiskaia istoriia* 4 (2011): 44–52; and Astashov, *Russkii front v 1914-nachale 1917 goda: voennyi opyt i sovremennost'* (Moscow: Novyi Khronogrof, 2014).

[28] The Bolsheviks were a communist party led by Vladimir Lenin, originally the Russian Social Democratic Labor Party, who led the second revolution to overthrow the Provisional Government in November 1917 (October according to the old Russian calendar, and thus the reason it is often termed the "October Revolution").

full year after the start of the war, he seemed to have no knowledge of the processes of conscription and the protests that accompanied mobilization that reflected serious discontent; the lack of identification with the empire's war aims on the part of millions of peasant soldiers; the tremendous problems associated with industrial organization, supply, and distribution; the devastating defeats suffered by the Russian army in that first year; or any problems faced by the army, such as fraternization with the enemy, voluntary surrender, desertion, or insubordination. He also seemed to have little idea of the pressures on soldiers and their families. He did come into contact with the latter, after the February Revolution, when he mentioned soldiers getting letters from home complaining about the hardships their families were facing without their labor participation. But he never seemed to make a connection between the suffering of the Russian people and the desire for revolution. In fact, his commentary about the shortages of food and the scarcity and inflation of necessities on the home front seems to suggest that these were effects, rather than causes, of revolt. He was not in Russia when either revolution occurred, and spent little time in the capital, Petrograd, where political events were unfolding. He also wrote his story immediately upon returning to the US, the finished product appearing in March 1918, before the outbreak of the Russian Civil War. Nonetheless, it is highly doubtful that he would have been oblivious to such important aspects of the revolutionary year. One might assume that he intentionally avoided discussing what he could have perceived as controversial issues. Since one of his goals was to convince an American audience that the Russian contribution to the war was a worthy one, he might not have wanted to touch on subject matter that put them in an unfavorable light, considering the virulent anti-Bolshevik sentiment that prevailed in many American circles.

Despite his biases and the shortcomings of his vision, Grow never lost faith in the Russians and continued to believe that the sacrifices they made during the war were not in vain. His descriptions of the action he saw and his role as a medical worker provide us with detailed accounts that reveal much about the experience of participation in mechanized total war. He was distinctly pro-Russian, even if he was overly optimistic. He was heartened by the entry of the United States into the conflict and was certain this would turn the tide in favor of the Entente. His narrative stops short, however, before the Russians withdrew from the conflict in early 1918. One can only wonder what his reaction to this decision would have been. The book nevertheless provides an interesting glimpse into the trials and tribulations that Russia faced during the war. One does get a strong sense of the serious obstacles the country faced in attempting to wage a total war, particularly the challenges involved with industrial warfare, its destructive effect on the human body, and its impact on Russia in this pivotal moment of its history. Therefore, it is a valuable resource in our attempts to further understand the complexities of Russia's Great War and Revolution.

Suggested Further Reading

Gatrell, Peter. *Russia's First World War: A Social and Economic History*. London: Pearson, 2005.

———. *A Whole Empire Walking*. Bloomington: Indiana University Press, 1999.

Golovin, Nikolai N. *The Russian Army in the World War*. New Haven, CT: Yale University Press, 1931.

Fuller, William C. *The Foe Within: Fantasies of Treason and the End of Imperial Russia*. Ithaca, NY: Cornell University Press, 2006.

Hutchinson, John. *Politics and Public Health in Revolutionary Russia, 1890–1918*. Baltimore: Johns Hopkins University Press, 1990.

Jahn, Hubertus F. *Patriotic Culture in Russia during World War I*. Ithaca, NY: Cornell University Press, 1995.

Lohr, Eric. "The Russian Army and the Jews: Mass Deportation, Hostages, and Violence during World War I." *The Russian Review* 60 (2001): 404–19.

Rachamimow, Alon. *POWs and the Great War: Captivity on the Eastern Front*. New York: Berg Publishers, 2002.

Sanborn, Joshua. *Imperial Apocalypse: The Great War and the Destruction of the Russian Empire*. New York: Oxford University Press, 2015.

———. *Drafting the Russian Nation: Military Conscription, Total War, and Mass Politics, 1905–1925*. DeKalb: Northern Illinois University Press, 2003.

Siegelbaum, Lewis H. *The Politics of Industrial Mobilization in Russia, 1914–1917: A Study of the War-Industries Committees*. New York: St. Martin's Press, 1983.

Snively, Major H. H. "Base Hospital Work in Russia." *The Military Surgeon: Journal of the Association of Military Surgeons of the United States* 38, no. 1 (1916): 623–32.

Stoff, Laurie S. *Russia's Sisters of Mercy and the Great War: More than Binding Men's Wounds*. Lawrence: University Press of Kansas, 2015.

Stoff, Laurie S. et al., eds. *Military Affairs in Russia's Great War and Revolution, 1914–1922, Book 1: Military Experiences*. Russia's Great War & Revolution Series. Bloomington, IN: Slavica, 2019.

Stone David R. *The Russian Army in the Great War: The Eastern Front 1914–1917*. Lawrence: University Press of Kansas, 2015.

Stone, Norman. *The Eastern Front, 1914–1917*. New York: Scribners, 1975.

Wildman, Allan K. *The End of the Russian Imperial Army: The Old Army and the Soldiers' Revolt*. Princeton, NJ: Princeton University Press, 1980.

———. *The End of the Russian Imperial Army, Volume II: The Road to Soviet Power and Peace*. Princeton, NJ: Princeton University Press, 1987.

SURGEON GROW

AN AMERICAN IN THE RUSSIAN FIGHTING

BY

MALCOLM C. GROW

Formerly Lieut.-Colonel Imperial Russian Army Medical Corps

NEW YORK
FREDERICK A. STOKES COMPANY
PUBLISHERS

Copyright, 1918, by
FREDERICK A. STOKES COMPANY

All rights reserved, including that of translation into foreign languages

TO

THE HONORABLE RAY BAKER
FORMERLY SECRETARY TO THE AMERICAN AMBASSADOR TO RUSSIA
NOW DIRECTOR OF THE UNITED STATES MINT

ALSO TO

COLONEL A. E. KALPASCHNECOFF
GENERAL MICHAEL PLESCHCOFF

AND

MY OTHER RUSSIAN FRIENDS

FOREWORD

One hot July day in 1917, on a road a couple of miles back of the Russian trenches,[1] I witnessed an incident which was to me one of the most significant in all my Russian experience.

It was just when the Russian offensive, the plan of which was conceived and carried out by the Kerensky government,[2] was beginning to break down.[3] The revolutionary soldiers had gone forward in their attacks when ordered to do so, but their morale was bad and when the Germans counter-attacked, the line gave way at a certain point. Wild rumors were circulated by pro-German tools who were in the Russian ranks. They cried out that the German cavalry was surrounding them, and caused a panic among the Russians, who turned and fled.

I was standing by the roadside talking to a British officer who was about to bring up his armored cars to get into action against the Germans. Several of these armored car sections had been sent by the British to Russia to give what help they could. The officer had ridden ahead of his motors to investigate the condition of the roads. As we

---

[1] Grow served with the 1st Siberian Army Corps. In the summer of 1917, this corps was located on the Russian Western Front, southeast of Vilnius (in present-day Lithuania). However, later in his narrative, Grow indicates that he was in Siberia on a mission for the Red Cross in July 1917, and only returned to the front in August of that year. So there is some doubt as to whether he witnessed this firsthand or related a story that he had heard.

[2] This was the Provisional Government that took power after the fall of the tsarist system in Russia following the February Revolution of 1917. Alexander Kerensky, the only socialist member of the newly-formed government, was initially appointed minister of justice, but then became minister of war and finally, in July of that year, prime minister. Thus, the government is sometimes referred to as the "Kerensky Government."

[3] The Kerensky (often also known as the June or July) Offensive was a plan of attack aimed at striking a final blow against the Germans and Austrians in order to allow Russia to withdraw from the war without having to incur the heavy territorial losses sustained previously during the war. Heavily pressured by its allies, Britain and France, to remain in the war, the new Russian Provisional Government, which had come to power in the aftermath of the February Revolution that brought down the tsarist regime, hoped this offensive would end Russia's involvement "honorably." For more on this, see Allan Wildman, *The End of the Russian Imperial Army, Volume II: The Road to Soviet Power and Peace* (Princeton, NJ: Princeton University Press, 1987), and Louise Erwin Heenan, *Russian Democracy's Fatal Blunder: The Summer Offensive of 1917* (New York: Praeger, 1987).

stood talking the roll of drums, crackles of rifles and machine-gun fire could be heard from our position.

Suddenly the British officer grasped my arm and pointing down the road in the direction of the trenches, exclaimed, "My word, old chap! What is raising that cloud of dust?"

A great yellow cloud rose in the air, sweeping towards us rapidly. I thought of artillery limbers coming back for more shells, but the volume of that cloud was too great. As it rolled nearer we made out a great straggling disorganized mob of soldiers, running for their lives, apparently. Many were without hats or coats and some had thrown their rifles away.

They were a panic-stricken mob bent only on putting as much space between themselves and the Germans as possible. Their grimy faces were streaked with sweat, their eyes glared wildly like the eyes of a stampeding herd of steers, as they bore down upon us.

When they were about a hundred feet from us the dapper little English lieutenant stepped into the middle of the road, raised his walking stick aloft with his left hand and held out his right hand with the gesture of a traffic-policeman stopping a runaway horse.

The frightened soldiers in the foremost ranks of the fleeing mob checked their pace, those in the rear crowded on. I expected to see them sweep that little khaki-clad figure aside like a straw, or trample him under foot. There were no Russian officers in sight. I thought they might have murdered any officers who had tried to stop their flight and I expected to see the Englishman go down with a bullet or a bayonet in his chest. Strange to say the entire crowd of nearly 500 men stopped before that dapper little figure with the outstretched arms. They stood stock still, their great burly chests heaving, their brown faces shining with moisture.

There was a strange silence for a moment, the thunder of pounding boots on hard earth had ceased and only the deep roll of artillery reached my ears. Then a clear, almost boyish voice began speaking in very bad Russian. The little officer told those Russians what he thought of them, what cowards they were to be running away, and ordered them to return and fight. It was not a very grammatical speech but it was forceful and liberally interspersed with good English "cuss words." The mob stood silently listening, many with a shamefaced expression. They crowded up nearer to hear, they forgot their panic of a moment before. When he finished speaking a scattered cheer which soon grew into a lusty roar from 500 throats boomed out. Several underofficers[4] and soldiers said a few words and in a trice they had formed into an orderly body in columns of eight and were marching back toward the battlefield. Those who had thrown their rifles away picked them up again and returned and fought like demons.

---

[4] Non-commissioned officers (NCOs).

FOREWORD

Had that officer been a Russian he would have been killed in an instant, but the mere fact that he was a foreigner saved the situation. The Russian soldier has a great respect for the French, the English and the American. Especially is the American looked up to, and it is astonishing the influence that can be wielded by one of our country men. The Russian is a simple-minded, childlike individual, but he is also an idealist and at heart he loves his fellowmen. Being primitive, his passions, either of love or hate, admiration or scorn, are naturally colossal. He is also sensitive to extraneous influences, as witness the effect of German propaganda.[5]

He is, and will be in the future, just as susceptible to the sympathy or criticism of the American people. At this time he needs help, he needs sympathy and above all he needs understanding. We will gain nothing by adverse criticism, but should reap much benefit both now at this very critical time in our national existence and in after years if we pursue the proper course toward Russia.

I have given a few lectures on Russia in the United States and have been struck by the division of feeling towards the Russian soldier. One attitude is of distinct and decided contempt; the other is a real appreciation of what he has done in the past for the Allies, and of the great sacrifice he has made for our cause, with a warm expression of sympathy for his present helpless and pitiable condition.

The book I have written contains no argument. I have tried to tell the simple story of what I saw, to relate my own experiences and impressions in a purely narrative style, leaving the reader to draw his own conclusions. My earnest desire is to bring plainly before the American people the heroic fight these peasant soldiers put up while suffering under most adverse conditions in the field and while many baneful influences were at work in the rear, undermining the organization of the Russian government and military machine.

Not only does Russia need our help at this time but I think all will agree that we need Russia's help.

Surely there should be a bond of sympathy between this the oldest, and Russia the youngest democracy,[6] and a united front against Prussian autocracy and militarism.

M. C. G.
Media, Pa., March 22, 1918.

---

[5] Grow's comments about Russian soldiers are consistent with stereotypes held both inside and outside of the country.

[6] Upon the fall of tsarism in February/March 1917, Russia was proclaimed a social democracy. However, by the time of his writing this foreword, March 1918, Russia had experienced a second revolution, wherein the Bolsheviks, a communist party, had taken power.

Chapter I
I GO TO RUSSIA

Dr. Edward Egbert,[1] of Washington, D.C., had not been as persuasive a talker as he was skilled as a surgeon, the most eventful eighteen months of my life would, I suppose, have been passed instead in the humdrum pursuit of my profession as a Philadelphia physician.

As a physician, I would have followed with more than average interest the great drama then being unfolded in Europe, because warfare, with all its pain and suffering, makes a special appeal to medical men, but my part, like that of the bulk of Americans, would have been that of a sympathizing onlooker rather than that of an active participant. At any rate, not until the United States had entered the war would it seriously have occurred to me to disrupt my personal affairs to take a part in a struggle in which we were but remotely interested.

As it was, however, the whole aspect of things, as far as I was concerned, was changed by a remarkable conversation I had with Dr. Egbert in Washington in August, 1915. That interview threw me into the great struggle almost as suddenly as Europe herself became engulfed in it. Some eight months before, Dr. Egbert had sailed from this country for Russia to become chief surgeon of the American Red Cross hospital at Kiev.[2] He was home again on a short leave of absence and planned to return within a few weeks.

We were in the Hotel Willard in Washington. It was a typical sultry August evening and we were seated by an open window although all the air we got came in the form of hot gusts from the street, bringing with them the shrill calls of newsboys, the honking of motor-car horns and the rattle of the street-cars.

As Dr. Egbert described to me some of the conditions prevailing on the Russian front, however, and the terrible things he had seen and undergone, I ceased to notice

---

[1] Egbert was an American surgeon who served as the chief surgeon of the American Red Cross Hospital, in Kiev, Ukraine (which was part of the Russian Empire), during the war, and executive secretary of the Catherine Breshkovsky Russian Relief Fund in New York.

[2] The hospital had been established in 1914 in the Kiev Polytechnic Institute. For more on the role of the American Red Cross in Russia, particularly in this hospital during the Great War, see Major H. H. Snively, "Base Hospital Work in Russia," *The Military Surgeon: Journal of the Association of Military Surgeons of the United States* 38, no. 1 (1916): 623–32.

the sounds of the busy city. His story carried me to war-torn Galicia and before my eyes passed a stream of wrecked humanity, straggling back through the dusky forest isles from the field of battle which lay at their farther border.

I could hear the cries of the wounded, the screeching of the shells and the rattle of the machine-guns and rifles.

"When I was over there this spring," the doctor told me, "I saw thousands of wounded sent back to the evacuation hospitals[3] with only the care which could be given them by orderlies—men who, it is true, had received a few months' training but who lacked any real knowledge of modem aseptic methods in the treatment of the wounded. "Just think," he continued, "the Russian regiments number four thousand, and sometimes after a fight a bare few hundred come back unscathed, perhaps a thousand being killed and the balance—more than two thousand—being more or less seriously wounded—and the regiment has just three doctors![4] What possible chance have three doctors to give proper attention to more than two thousand cases in the space of the few hours at their disposal!"

This was a revelation to me. I had no idea that any of the armies in the great conflict were so poorly equipped with medical men.[5]

"As you know," the doctor went on, "I was in charge of the hospital at Kiev. When these poor fellows reached me after journeying for perhaps three or four days from the front their condition was pitiable. Many of them still had on the original first aid dressings which the orderlies had applied on the battle-field and in a great percentage of the cases the delay in administering proper medical attention had resulted disastrously.

---

[3] According to Russian military medical procedures, wounded soldiers received immediate medical attention at the front to stabilize them enough to be sent to the rear to be treated more fully in hospitals outside of the war zone.

[4] The Russian Imperial Army had fewer than 12,000 doctors serving the troops during the Great War. In addition, over 31,000 nurses and 60,000 medics/orderlies carried out medical services.

[5] The Russian government had not anticipated the vast number of medical personnel, facilities, equipment, and supplies that would be required to successfully wage a world war. The extensive scale of the war coupled with the lack of experience and reluctance to utilize civilian sources of support often hindered efficient provision of medical services and proved troublesome for the Russian Armed Forces, which suffered very high casualties. By September 1917, the number of Russian troops wounded in the war was approximately 2.5 million. Nearly one million died of their wounds. Another 2.3 million soldiers had fallen ill as a result of the spread of highly contagious epidemic diseases, including typhoid fever, typhus, cholera, and dysentery, as well as other illnesses such as pneumonia or scurvy. See John F. Hutchinson, *Politics and Public Health in Revolutionary Russia, 1890–1918* (Baltimore: Johns Hopkins University Press, 1990); *Rossiia v mirovoi voine*; and Peter Gatrell, *Russia's First World War: A Social and Economic History* (Harlow, England: Pearson Education Limited, 2005).

"Grow, Russia needs doctors and needs them badly. There is no time to lose. We must forget all questions of race or nationality and remember only that we are doctors and are able to avert some of the awful suffering which our fellow human-beings are compelled to endure for the want of the attention which we can provide. How about your going over with me, Grow?"

I must confess that the doctor's eloquence had deeply impressed me, but not until he put the question to me flatly had I sensed its personal application.

"If you will come with me, Grow, when I sail two weeks from to-day," the doctor continued, noticing my hesitation, "you'll never regret it, I can assure you. I'm going on the Russian munition ship *Dvinsk* from New York, and if you'll go with me I'm quite sure you won't have the slightest difficulty in obtaining a commission in the Russian army medical service. You will gain there an experience in surgery in a few months which you could not get otherwise in years and years of private practice.

"I don't know, but we all feel—all of us who are in Europe—that America is bound to be drawn into this great world conflict. If we do come in, the training and experience which you will get in Russia will stand you in good stead when the opportunity comes to serve your own country.

"Aside from that—think of the help you will be to suffering humanity. The satisfaction you will derive from that in after years will more than repay you for the time you devote to this work. Will you come?"

The surgeon's eyes glowed with enthusiasm. He was a very different man from the one I had known some eight months before. It was not so much the lines of care in his face as it was something else which I cannot describe. As it was, as I looked earnestly into his face I realized that the part he had played in the great war had made him better and stronger than when I had last seen him.

I made a sudden decision. I resolved to go to Russia. I would throw up my practice, sail with Dr. Egbert two weeks hence, and try to get a commission in the Russian army. The doctor's eloquence had awakened in me an inherent love of adventure, a latent desire to see this great world tragedy, and a growing belief that the experience which I would gain in Russia would prove of some benefit to my own country later on.

That was in the latter part of August, 1915. Just one month later, Dr. Egbert and I drove down the Morskaya in Petrograd, swung round the corner into St. Isaac's square, over whose cobblestones our *droshky*[6] clattered, and halted in front of our hotel opposite the great cathedral.

This hotel, the Astoria, was situated on the square. It was a large brownstone building, built and owned by a German company but taken over by the Russian government after war was declared.

We arrived about tea-time and the lobby was filled with a brilliant throng of officers and ladies. An orchestra was playing, and save for the presence of officers with

---

[6] A low, two- or four-wheeled carriage.

arms in slings and others who walked on crutches, one could scarcely have realized that it was war-time.[7]

I shall always remember my first dinner in the Astoria. Dr. Egbert and myself were the guests of several Americans who were stopping there. At one end of the beautiful dining-room of the hotel was a long counter upon which was displayed all manner of *zachowsky*,[8] caviar, smoked fish of every description, mushrooms pickled in vinegar, shrimp, crawfish, etc. White-garbed attendants served whatever was selected, which was eaten right there or taken to the table. Then followed a typical Russian dinner of cabbage soup, trout, quail, roast veal, various vegetables, artichokes, dessert and tea—a remarkable contrast to the foodless banquets which have since become to [sic] prevalent all over the world.

It was a brilliant assemblage. At a small table on our right was the Grand Duke Michael[9] with a party of friends. He was a slender chap, about thirty-six years of age. His hair was close cropped and he wore the uniform of a captain of Hussars. At other tables were Cossack officers with their picturesque, many-colored uniforms, silver-handled sabres and daggers, with revolvers on their hips, dark swarthy faces and glowing black eyes, lending color and atmosphere to the scene.

When a general, his breast covered with crosses and other decorations, would enter the room, every officer of lower rank would rise from his table, click his spurs together and bow, the general bowing in return and the officers standing facing him until he was seated.

The women were superb in their Parisian gowns, and I had never seen such jewels. A vivacious conversation was general and there was much laughter. French was spoken more than Russian.

This picture is so vastly different from that which I saw some fourteen months later when I returned to Russia after a short visit home—during which time the Czar had been deposed—that, at the cost of digressing, I can't help referring to it.

I found that the Astoria had been wrecked by the Revolutionists. The dining-room was a shambles. Officers no longer kept up their appearance or bearing and the few who dined in the soiled, bedraggled room, presided over by insolent, slovenly

---

[7] The lavish lifestyles of Russia's elite were the cause of much discontent on the part of the country's masses, who suffered from serious economic problems during the war, including shortages of basic necessities and high inflation. See, for example, W. Bruce Lincoln, *Passage Through Armageddon: The Russians in War and Revolution, 1914–1918* (New York: Oxford University Press, 1994).

[8] Appetizers.

[9] Grand Duke Mikhail Aleksandrovich (1878–1918), Tsar Nicholas II's youngest brother. He commanded the Caucasian Cavalry (or "Savage") Division during World War I. When Nicholas abdicated after the February Revolution in 1917, he did so in favor of his brother Mikhail, but the latter refused the throne.

Tartar[10] waiters, ate silently, with gloomy, hopeless faces, brooding over the chaos which surrounded them and addressing the waiters in the most respectful tones lest they be refused service.

But to return to my first visit to Petrograd. After dinner, Dr. Egbert met in the lobby a young officer acquaintance, Captain Dumbrofsky, who spoke English and from whom I got the first inkling of what was going on in Russia as a result of German propaganda.

Captain Dumbrofsky's right arm was bandaged and carried in a sling and he looked fagged and worn.

"It has been terrible!" he exclaimed. "We have been steadily retreating for two months. Our soldiers have fought magnificently, holding trenches until whole regiments have been simply wiped out by the Nemets (German) long range heavy artillery. My own regiment has been all but annihilated—all my comrades are killed or wounded."

"How is it that you have been unable to hold them?" I asked.

"The trouble has been," the Captain explained, a little shamefacedly, "we have no equipment. Our men have had to fight with clubs and stones. Our field artillery, the guns of which can fire eighteen shells per minute, were allowed for many days only three shells per day for each gun!"[11]

We asked him what his personal plans were.

"I am only slightly wounded," he replied, "and hope to return to the front in a few days. I cannot stay here in Petrograd while my country is being invaded."

He looked a fit subject for a hospital and I told him I thought he should not return too soon.

"*Nichevo!* It is nothing!" he said. "I am quite well and strong, and my place is at the front."

"They are nearly all like that," Dr. Egbert explained to me as we walked away; "they simply don't know what quit means."

My subsequent experiences fully confirmed the doctor's view.

---

[10] Turkic-speaking peoples originating in the Mongol Empire who came to Russia through the mass migrations of the 13th–15th centuries, but long residing in Russia.

[11] The shell (and concomitant rifle) shortage of 1915 was the result of poor planning for the scale of the war and poor coordination between private industry and government. See Norman Stone, *The Eastern Front, 1914–1917* (New York: Scribners, 1975), 144–64. However, as he, as well as David R. Stone (no relation) in his more recent work *The Russian Army in the Great War: The Eastern Front 1914–1917* (Lawrence: University Press of Kansas, 2015), indicates, these problems were in no way unique to the armies of the countries fighting this war.

Chapter II
TWO WEEKS OF SIGHT-SEEING

The next morning we were up early. One of the first things we did was to pay a visit to Henry, one of our fellow-passengers on the voyage from America to Russia.

Henry was a little mouse-like man, who had never been a hundred miles from the small seaport town in New England which was his home. Henry had been employed all his life with a shipbuilding company. This company had built some submarine-chasers for the Russian government but for some reason or other they refused to chase. The motors wouldn't go and the vessels were lying in the Gulf of Finland, near Kronstadt, waiting for the magic touch of someone from the shipbuilding company, and Henry had been delegated to apply it.

"There's something wrong with the hot-water tap in my bathroom," complained Henry, as we entered his room, which was on the floor below ours. "I've tinkered with the durned thing for an hour but I can't get it to work."

"Well, why don't you get the hall porter to fix it for you?" suggested Dr. Egbert. "You'll find him out there by the elevator."

Henry went out and in a moment or two returned with a uniformed man who, to say the least, seemed most reluctant to help Henry solve the problem of the hot-water tap. Indeed, if Henry had not dragged him forcibly by the arm, he certainly wouldn't have entered the room at all. "I want you to fix the hot-water tap," Henry explained, holding the rebellious official with one hand and pointing to the bathroom with the other. Right then it occurred to me that something was very much amiss. The old gentleman whom Henry had dragged into his room looked as if he were going to have an apoplectic fit, and a glance I got at Dr. Egbert showed me that he was almost in as precarious a condition.

With an indignant snort, Henry's prisoner tore himself from his captor's grasp and rushed from the room with Henry in pursuit.

"Great Scott, Henry!" shouted Dr. Egbert. "Come back, will you! That's not the porter; that's an admiral of the Russian Navy!"

Henry's jaw fell and he almost collapsed. "You've got yourself in dutch now, for fair," Dr. Egbert went on. "You've gravely insulted him, and the chances are he'll have you thrown into prison."

"But I thought he was the porter—with all that gold braid and stuff—and he was standing at the elevator, too," replied Henry, whose face had turned the color of ashes.

Just then a dapper little fellow in the blue uniform of a naval lieutenant knocked at the door and, in a very correct English, declared:

"The Admiral demands an apology from the American who has so gravely insulted him!"

Henry being quite speechless, Dr. Egbert explained the cause of the supposed affront and offered Henry's profuse apologies to the Admiral. The Lieutenant clanked his heels together, saluted, and solemnly withdrew. After a few moments he returned with the information that the Admiral would accept the apologies of the American—a message which undoubtedly saved Henry's life, because I fully believe another five minutes of suspense would have killed him.

The incident was an amusing one to me; but Henry's mistake was really quite excusable because of the fact that in Russia everyone wears some sort of uniform, even the school children, and one has to live in Russia quite a while before understanding the significance of all the different uniforms which are worn.

After breakfast, Dr. Egbert suggested that we go sight-seeing, and I gladly acquiesced.

After considerable haggling with an *isvoscheek*,[1] or cabman, in front of the hotel—a most necessary preliminary—we piled into the rickety old cab and went clattering off over the cobblestones of St. Isaac's Square.

These *isvoscheeks* are droll looking fellows, with great padded coats fastened around the waist by a tight belt. The more costly the equipage and the finer the horse, the greater the padding, and the fare seemed to vary in direct ratio with the amount of padding—an *isvoscheek* who looked as though he could roll more easily than walk charging two or three times as much as a more slender one.

They were usually bearded and wore quaint high hats and altogether they presented a very weird appearance—especially if the face and neck were thin and scrawny in contrast to the hugely padded body. Some were mere boys of fourteen or fifteen, but all wore the quaint top hat, no matter how battered or frayed, and the huge padded coat.

We passed a long column of men marching four abreast, with an armed guard of soldiers escorting them. They were raw youths in every conceivable costume—a draft of new troops called up for training. They ambled and slouched along carrying bundles and packages, shuffling in their heavy boots—typical country bumpkins.[2]

"How can they ever make soldiers out of such material?" I asked.

---

[1] *Izvozchik*.

[2] The vast majority of the Russian Imperial Army were conscripted peasants.

"Well, there's the answer," replied Dr. Egbert, pointing ahead of us, "those soldiers you see marching towards us were an exact counterpart of these fellows only a few weeks ago."

I looked in the direction he indicated and saw a long, orderly line of soldiers in grey-brown marching towards us in perfect rhythm, with the free swing of the Russian military step, their heavy hobnailed boots thumping the cobblestones in absolute time. Fine erect soldierly men they were, every slender bayonetted rifle at the same angle, every movement in unison.

We stopped a moment as they passed us. The officer's voice could be heard ringing out with bell-like clearness, a great church we were passing acting as a sounding-board, as he addressed an order to his men, then a metallic clatter as every rifle-butt hit the cobblestones together.

Our *isvoscheek* took us through the great wide thoroughfare called the Nevsky Prospect. As wide as it was, both sidewalks and road-bed were very crowded and our *isvoscheek* had constantly to yell at unwary pedestrians who got in our way, rattling his whip in the socket and waving his arm to urge the horse on.

The buildings were immense solid-looking structures, some of stone but many of stucco. They had been painted yellow or reddish brown but most of them were faded and dingy and looked in need of a new coat.

Most of the men we passed were in uniform.

One of the peculiarities I noticed was the fact that practically every shop in addition to a sign giving the name of the firm and the commodity handled had a picture of the commodity painted on the walls—a baker's shop having loaves of bread, rolls and cakes painted above the windows, a furniture store chairs, tables, couches and side boards, and so on.

This was done, Dr. Egbert explained, because seventy percent of the population could not read and lettered signs meant nothing to them.[3] While this revelation of the proportion of illiteracy in Russia was appalling, it was rather consoling to me to reflect that the ignorance of the natives would make shopping easier for me.

Altogether I spent two weeks in sight-seeing, and very interesting weeks they were. I had many wonderful drives through the islands. There were dinners at Felician's on the balcony overlooking the canal where boats carrying students rowing with their sweethearts in the crisp October evenings would float by, the silence broken by beautiful youthful voices singing the sad romances the Russian loves so well.

Meanwhile, of course, I was watching for an opportunity to enter the Russian army medical service. The fact that I did not speak Russian and had no friends in

---

[3] The literacy rate in pre-Revolutionary Russia is a matter of some debate, but has been estimated between 20 and 40% by the turn of the nineteenth century. See Ben Eklof, "Russian Literacy Campaigns 1861–1939," in *National Literacy Campaigns and Movements: Historical and Comparative Perspectives*, ed. Robert F. Arnove and Harvey J. Graff (New Brunswick, NJ: Transaction, 2008), 128–29.

the Russian army made the task extremely difficult, but finally I heard, through an American acquaintance, of a Russian surgeon who was anxious to go away to Finland for a vacation. He had been working day and night since the beginning of the war and was nearly broken down from the strain of overwork.

Securing a letter of introduction from the American, I called on this surgeon, Dr. Vicker, at his office.

Dr. Vicker was a charming man, of middle age, with a scar from cheek bone to chin from a sabre cut received while a student in Germany.

He explained to me that he was chief surgeon to the Hussars[4] Hospital at Tsarskoe Selo,[5] which had a hundred and fifty beds, and he was also attending a large private practice. He was doing all of the surgical work, having only a woman doctor[6] in the hospital, who acted as anesthetist and resident physician, to help him. The fighting was intense at that time, October, 1915, and they were crowded with work.

"I shall be very glad, Dr. Grow," he declared, after a short interview in which I told him of my professional experience in America, "to have you come with me tomorrow to Tsarskoe Selo and help me with several operations. I can then judge of your ability and you will become familiar with our work. Meet me, if you will, at the Tsarskoe Selo Station at Petrograd at seven o'clock tomorrow morning."

Delighted with the opportunity to do some work, I thanked him for his interest and promised to be on hand in time. Sight-seeing was very interesting, but I had left America to work in Russia, not to enjoy myself, and I was very anxious to start in.

---

[4] Light cavalry units.

[5] The Romanov tsar's summer residence.

[6] Russia was one of the first countries to allow women to obtain medical degrees, beginning in the mid-nineteenth century. For more on women doctors in pre-Revolutionary Russia, see Christine Johanson, "Autocratic Politics, Public Opinion, and Women's Medical Education During the Reign of Alexander II, 1855–1881," *Slavic Review* 38, no. 3 (1979): 426–43, and Jeanette E. Tuve, *The First Russian Women Physicians* (Newtonville, MA: Oriental Research Partners, 1984).

Chapter III
THE HUSSARS HOSPITAL AT TSARSKOE-SELO

A forty-five minute ride by train from Petrograd brought us to Tsarskoe Selo which literally means the village of the Czar. It was so called because the Emperor had his favorite palace there, where he spent most of his time before he became commander-in-chief of the Russian Armies in the field, when he removed to Mogheliv,[1] where the General Staff was located. We engaged a droshky and drove to the hospital, passing some of the beautiful grounds surrounding the palace.

The hospital was a large white structure, used in peace times as the special hospital of the Hussars, a large body of whom are permanently stationed at Tsarskoe Selo. On the ground floor was the receiving room and two large airy wards with rows of white cots all occupied by wounded soldiers.

On the second floor was the officers' ward, an operating room and dressing room, baths, etc.; while the third floor was divided into small private rooms for cases requiring isolation and quiet, and the rooms for the resident doctor and several resident nurses.

All the nurses except one were titled women who, at the beginning of the war, had taken the six months' training course required to become a war-sister.[2] They had given up everything else and devoted themselves resolutely to the task in hand.

The exception was a lady who had been a professional nurse for many years, and who acted as assistant in operations and had charge of the operating room.

I met the head sister, Baroness Maria Alexandrovna P——, a fine motherly woman of fifty-five, with snow-white hair and the sweetest face imaginable, and the ten other sisters, all of whom were either Baronesses or Princesses with the exception of the little professional nurse, who was simply Sister Olga Michaelovna.

---

[1] Mogilev, headquarters of the Russian General Staff, or *Stavka*, located in present-day eastern Belarus.

[2] Nursing service became a very popular means for women to contribute to the war effort, and many of Russia's elite women, as well as those from middle and working classes, volunteered for medical duties. To meet the high demand for nursing personnel, training courses were quickly shortened to two months, and subsequently, to six weeks. Assignment to the hospital at Tsarskoe Selo would have only been possible for the best-connected women of the Russian aristocracy. Others served in much less prestigious establishments, many very close to the fighting. For more on Russia's nurses during the war, see Stoff, *Russia's Sisters of Mercy*.

Let me digress for a moment to explain Russian names. In Russia persons are called by their first names and their middle names, which latter consists of the father's name to which, in a male, ovitch is added, and, in a female, ovna is added. Thus Olga Michaelovna signified Olga, the daughter of Michael. Even servants address their masters by the first two names, the family name being invariably omitted. The Grand Duke Nicholas is spoken of by everyone as Nicholi Nicholiovich.[3] All of the sisters spoke English perfectly, many of them having received their education in England and all having travelled and spent much time there. This was a great relief to me and in conjunction with the charming friendliness and courtesy with which I was received quickly put me at my ease.

Dr. Vicker led the way to the wash-room and we scrubbed up and donned sterile gowns.

Two operations were done: the first, a brain operation in which we evacuated and drained a large brain abscess; the second, an amputation at the thigh for gangrene.

Dr. Vicker was a skillful and dexterous surgeon and I have never seen finer work done. The sisters worked like veteran nurses and everything in the operating-room was like clock-work.

Next came the dressing of cases. They were wheeled in on stretchers by orderlies, and transferred to an operating table, where the bandages were removed, the wounds inspected and dressings applied.

Many of these wounds were horribly infected, and drainage tubes and gauze drains had to be removed and fresh ones inserted. I was astonished at the fortitude with which these men bore their pain. They would grip the hand of one of the kindly nurses until the muscles in their arms stood out like knots, and the sister would wince with pain from the pressure, but never a word of complaint came from the soldier. When asked if it hurt very much, the soldier would smile, although pallid and damp with agony, and reply: "*Nichevo!*" meaning, "It is nothing!"

Forty or fifty dressings were done and then we visited some cases which did not require dressings.

One of them was a case which had developed tetanus, or lockjaw, the day before. He had had a slight wound of the instep from a piece of high explosive shell. It had nearly healed when the dread symptom of lockjaw developed.

As we entered the little room in which he was isolated, his body was arched like a bent bow, resting on his heels and the back of his head, his face drawn into a ghastly grin, the teeth exposed the expression sardonic. This convulsion lasted a long time and gradually relaxed but not completely. At the slightest noise or a sudden movement, the condition would be repeated.

---

[3] Nikolai Nikolaiovich.

"A terrible thing this," the doctor whispered. "We haven't enough serum to give a prophylactic dose to all our wounded as they do in France, and I have had four cases in this hospital, all of which have died."

I inquired as to the amount of anti-tetanic serum they were using in the treatment and found that it was infinitesimal—only 11,500 units—as compared with the doses used in America, and was injected only under the skin.

"May I try the treatment we use in America large doses into the spinal canal and veins?" I asked.

"Certainly," replied the doctor, "if we can secure such a large amount of serum, but we are allowed only a small quantity because the supply in Russia is so limited."[4]

I was determined to cure that man if it were possible; and after we had returned to Petrograd I called on one of the Americans I knew, who was travelling for one of our large manufacturing chemists.

"How much anti-tetanic serum have you, Philip?" I inquired.

"About a million units."

"May I have 500,000? I want it to save a case at the Hussars Hospital." And I explained to him the facts of the case.

"Why, certainly, Doctor," he replied. "I'll get it for you at once."

I boarded the next train to Tsarskoe Selo, with the precious serum in my kit. I gave the patient 100,000 units at once, part into the spinal column with a long hollow needle, and the rest into a vein.

The head nurse was astonished at the enormous dose and very skeptical as to the results, but I was hopeful, and was rewarded the next morning by a slight diminution in the severity and number of the convulsions. I repeated the dose, and the next day, when with Dr. Vicker I visited the patient, his improvement was quite noticeable.

A plump, rosy-cheeked little sister, the Princess Tatiana Alexandrovna,[5] had taken this poor fellow, a fine lad of about twenty-five, as her special charge. She had been tireless in her attention, and as I stood watching him I felt that in her I had a staunch ally in the desperate fight against death. I wasn't mistaken. I learned that with infinite patience and gentleness she had managed to separate the tightly locked jaws from time to time to allow some liquid nourishment to trickle, drop by drop, down the rigid throat, which the slightest disturbance was apt to throw into convulsions expelling the food.

We gave still another 100,000 units, and that evening I was informed by telephone of appreciable improvement in the patient's condition.

---

[4] Shortages of medical supplies, including medicines, were common in Russia during the Great War.

[5] Many women of the Russian aristocracy and royal family entered into nursing service during the war. Among those working at Tsarskoe Selo were the tsarina, Alexandra, and her two eldest daughters, Tatiana Nikolaevna and Olga Nikolaevna. It is not clear who this princess (Tatiana Alexandrovna) was.

The next day the dose was reduced to 30,000 units, and later to 10,000, which was continued for a week, by which time he had entirely recovered.

The recovery of this man gave me a prestige in the hospital which no amount of real hard work at dressings and operating table could have done. To a certain extent, it was what we call "playing to the grandstand." On the other hand, the man's life was saved, and that, of course, was the important thing. But I believe, after that, I could have made all manner of mistakes and still retained the respect and admiration of those sisters.

During the week that the tetanus case was being treated, I worked every day with Dr. Vicker, and he finally decided that I had become familiar enough with the work to carry it on alone, and he left for Finland, leaving me in charge.

We had received no new wounded since I began work, but on the contrary had been discharging some of the convalescent cases to be sent to special convalescent hospitals. The night after Dr. Vicker left, at 10 P.M., I received word by telephone at my hotel to come at once to Tsarskoe Selo, as new wounded were coming in.

Arriving at the hospital I found all the sisters hard at work cleaning up some forty soldiers who had just arrived. They had been four days in the train and many had not had their bandages changed since leaving the first aid stations near the firing line and had been bumped around all this time lying on straw in box cars.

They were naturally in a terrible condition muddy, covered with vermin, and many badly infected.

Of the forty, five had gangrenous phlegmon or gas bacillus infection so severe as to require immediate amputation, two below the knee, two at the thigh, and one at the wrist.

The task of getting them ready for operation was a nasty one. They had to be bathed, have their hair clipped and clean clothes put on, yet these women, not one of whom before the war had ever done a stroke of disagreeable work or even had to experience anything unpleasant, went about their tasks cheerfully and smiling, always gentle and kind, caring for those peasant soldiers as though they were their very own children.

I recall one old fellow who had a very large red beard. He was driver on a soup kitchen and had been hit on the head by a piece of shrapnel, producing a nasty scalp wound. It was necessary to clip his hair and beard short, as they were matted with blood and dirt. If we had decided to amputate his head he could not have put up more of a fight than when he observed that we were about to shave off his beard.[6]

After Baroness Maria Alexandrovna had talked to him for ten minutes as one would talk to a captious child, however, she won him over, although during the clip-

---

[6] The beard had special significance to Russian peasant men, both a symbol of religious devotion and of adulthood.

ping process tears came to the poor chap's eyes as he witnessed the massacre of his great flaming red beard—the pride of his simple life.

The busy weeks sped on and I became thoroughly engrossed in my work. At length, Dr. Vicker returned. He asked me to continue on as his assistant, but I had just heard of a man who had come up from the front looking for a surgeon and I was anxious to get into more active service. The man in question was Col. Kalpaschnecoff,[7] commander of the 21st Flying Column[8] attached to the First Siberian Army Corps. I had never heard of the Colonel before but I had heard of the famous corps to which he was attached. It had been christened the "Ironside Corps" because of its wonderful achievements in this war.[9] I left Tsarskoe Selo to offer myself to Col. Kalpaschnecoff.

---

[7] Andrei I. Kalpashnikov-Camac. See introduction for biographical information on Kalpashnikov.

[8] Flying columns (*letuchky*) were mobile medical units used by Russia's military medical services to treat wounded soldiers at the front as soon as possible. They consisted of transport vehicles such as horse-drawn carts and mobile dressing stations that allowed medical workers to move with the troops, as the nature of the war on the Eastern Front was much more mobile than that of the oft-static trench warfare associated with the Western Front during this conflict. The 21st Flying Column was supposedly funded by Countess Tolstoy, widow of the famed writer Lev.

[9] The 1st Siberian Army Corps was formed in 1900 as an elite force, serving with great distinction during the Russo-Japanese War (1904–05). During World War I, it was commanded by Lieutenant General Mikhail M. Pleshkov and consisted of the 1st and 2nd Siberian Rifle Divisions, the 1st and 2nd Siberian Artillery Battalions, the 1st Siberian Radio Battalion, 1st Siberian Ponton (Pontoon) Battalion, and the Ussuri Cavalry Brigade. It was dissolved in 1918.

Chapter IV
PREPARING TO GO TO THE FRONT

Through a war correspondent for an American newspaper who was stopping at the Astoria, a luncheon was arranged at which I was presented to Col. Kalpaschnecoff.

The Colonel proved to be a charming fellow. He had formerly been an attaché at the Russian Embassy in Washington, having left the diplomatic service at the outbreak of the war and been placed in command of the 21st Flying Column. "You'll find things pretty rough at the front," he said, in perfect English, his keen brown eyes searching my face. "The work is up in the first line trenches and things get rather hot occasionally. My surgeon was killed a few weeks ago."[1] I told him I wanted to see some action and was willing to take a chance, but I was afraid that my ignorance of the Russian language would prevent my getting a commission.

"I think we can get around that all right," the Colonel replied. "I have three medical students who will act as your assistants. One of them speaks English. Get a letter from the Hussars Hospital and bring your medical college diploma and we will go tomorrow to the Russian Red Cross and get you a commission in the Army medical service."

It sounded very easy and it looked as though at last my wish to get to the front was going to be realized.

Colonel Kalpaschnecoff was a whirlwind. His stay in Washington had evidently taught him American methods. He went to the Red Cross and walked through secretaries and clerks as though they were wet paper, literally brushing them aside as they tried to stop us to inquire our business, and before they had recovered we were in the presence of the all-powerful, and the Colonel was telling him that I was the man he wanted for his surgeon and that no other would do.

He had a glass of tea at his elbow on the desk. He asked the Colonel a few questions as to my ability, experience and credentials, and Kalpaschnecoff showed him the excellent letter from the heads of the Tsarskoe Selo Hospital, translated the heading of my diploma, and the trick was done.

---

[1] Being a medical worker in Russia during the Great War did not shield individuals from the dangers of combat, as medical units often worked on the front lines and came under enemy attack.

When it came to filling out the necessary blanks, I was asked whether my middle name—"Cummings"—was my father's name. When I told them that it was my grandfather's they decided that I would have to change it. My father's name was Alva and they thereupon rechristened me "Malcolm Alvaovitch Grow"!

"You will receive the commission of a captain," I was informed, "but being a foreigner it is customary to raise the rank one degree and you will wear the uniform of a *put-pulkovneck*."[2] The latter designation meant literally a lieutenant-colonel, which is the next rank above captain, there being no major in the Russian Army.

I expressed my surprise to the Colonel at the quickness with which he had carried off things.

"It's a trick I learned in America," he replied; "simply rush them off their feet. I told them you must have all your papers in three days as we leave for the front in five. Now you must get uniforms and equipment.[3] Here is a list you will need. Get busy and I will call at the hotel in a couple of days and see how you are getting on."

I drove back to the hotel rather dazed by the rapidity with which my destiny was rushing on. Here I was, a peace-loving American doctor stepping into the boots of a man killed two weeks ago by a German shell, thousands of miles from home and friends, with a commission in an army of strange folks with whom I must remain through unknown perils until such time as I might be "relieved of duty at the pleasure of the Army Command or until the end of the war"—so read the paper which I had just signed.

But that was what I had come over for and I was determined to see it through.

Arriving at the Astoria, I found Dr. Egbert just back from Kiev, the American Red Cross having withdrawn all its units from Europe because of lack of funds to maintain them.

"You lucky dog!" was the greeting I got from the doctor, when I told him of my good fortune. "I came over hoping to have work right at the front and they gave me a Base Hospital in a city, while you step right into the real thing.[4]

He told me he was going to remain in Petrograd a few weeks to settle up some business and then he was going back to America, which made me feel even more strongly the loneliness and isolation which were soon to be mine.

I had the tailor come to the hotel and I selected material for my uniform which he said he could have made up in three days.

Dr. Egbert and I went shopping and I purchased a huge curved sabre, as described on Kalpaschnecoff's list, several pairs of high black boots, and a funny Per-

---

[2] *Podpolkovnik*. The rank of major was eliminated in the Russian Imperial Army in 1884.

[3] Russian officers were responsible for acquiring uniforms and equipment themselves, at their own expense.

[4] The desire to work on the front lines rather than in medical facilities in the rear was common among medical workers in Russia during the Great War.

sian lamb cap, gray and high, the regulation winter cap for officers, worn cocked over the right ear. I also got a pair of nice jingly spurs.

During the next few days I watched the officers around the hotel rather closely. I had to learn just how to click my heels together when I saluted a superior or when I shook hands with an officer. The spurs produce a fine ringing sound which Dr. Egbert described as "singing with the feet." It was also necessary to learn not to salute when my hat was off—merely to bow and click my heels.

The hotel lobby was a very interesting and instructive place to sit at that period and I spent a great deal of time there. By observation I was soon able to familiarize myself with the insignia which went with the different ranks and the various branches of the service.

Several Americans dropped into my rooms for tea. Indicating my sheepskin coat hanging back of a curtain, one of them asked me if I were keeping a goat.

As a matter of fact, Kalpaschnecoff had told me that it was frequently from fifteen to twenty degrees below zero at the front in mid-winter and it was now the first of December.

It was certainly getting cold here in Petrograd. Furs were being worn by everyone and the short period of daylight lasting only from 9 A.M. to 3:30 P.M. told that the bleak cold gray days of the long Russian winter were upon us.

My uniforms finally came and I rigged myself out and went down to dinner, sabre and all, it being necessary to wear the weapon in official Petrograd although it could be dispensed with, strangely enough, at the front. I was grateful for the latter regulation, as the sabre was constantly getting between my legs and banging about in a very uncomfortable manner, my entry into the crowded cafe being a real menace to myself and others because of its tripping-up proclivities.

After dinner I started out to call on some friends to say good-bye. They had given their address on a piece of paper, written in Russian. I thought I remembered how my friend had pronounced it before he wrote it down and I walked boldly up to a bearded *isvoscheek* in front of the hotel and said, "Kee-roosh, naya, ad-een-nat-set!" and seated myself in the cab.

He clucked to his horses and started off and we drove for about an hour. Then he stopped and asked me something in Russian, which, of course, I couldn't answer. I handed him the slip of paper but he shook his head and handed it back to me. He couldn't read! I shook my head to indicate that I too was unable to read and he started off again at a walk, turning on the box from time to time to look at his strange fare—a Russian lieutenant-colonel who couldn't read!

Finally he saw a large policeman and drove up to him, saying something in Russian and pointing to me with his whip. I handed the paper to the policeman, who glanced at it, said something to the cabman and then burst into loud guffaws in which the cabman joined, both apparently overcome with mirth at the thought of a Russian officer of my rank who couldn't even read; and when later on, as a result of the policeman's directions, the cabman finally landed me at my friends' house and I dismissed him, he was still grinning and chuckling to himself.

I never understood why the policeman hadn't arrested me as a suspicious character.

The next day, Dr. Egbert accompanied me to the great, gloomy Nicholiavsky[5] station. The waiting-room was filled with a crowd of soldiers and officers with their families and friends seeing them off for the front.

Bearded, white-aproned *nasielshicks*,[6] or porters, ran up, and hand-baggage was piled into their waiting arms. We procured a couple of these porters and were soon headed for our train, following the porters, who staggered along under their seemingly impossible loads.

At the train, we met Kalpaschnecoff. He had managed to secure a compartment for two on the crowded second-class coach. I had my little regulation officer's trunk, filled with my effects, and my folding cot and bedding roll with blankets and pillows, carried in and piled in our compartment.

Then I went out on the platform where my dear old friend Dr. Egbert was standing. To me he represented the last link with life in America. "God bless you, boy!" he said, and there were tears in his eyes as he said it. There were tears in mine, too, and I suppose there were few on that platform whose eyes were dry, for it was a train running direct to the front and the passengers were all soldiers. How many of us would ever return?

As I stepped aboard, Dr. Egbert handed me a revolver in a soiled leather holster.

"Here, Grow," he said, "take this: it is a good gun. I have had it for a long time. It will not fail you. I want you to have it—from me."

I did not realize then what a friend that old thirty-eight was to prove, but it saved my life one blood-stained day on the Galician front—but more of that later on.

---

[5] Nikolaevsky.

[6] *Nosil'shchik*.

Chapter V
OFF TO THE FRONT

As we sat in our little compartment in the train before retiring, Col. Kalpaschnecoff explained to me the working details of the Column to which I was to be attached.

They had thirty-five horse-drawn ambulances, and equipment for three first-aid dressing stations. They worked in the First Division of the First Siberian Army Corps. Advanced dressing stations were established in the trenches, and there was a larger station somewhat farther back where the ambulances could come up. This station was usually one-half to one mile from the firing line. The wounded were carried from the advance dressing station to the main dressing station by stretcher bearers and from there they were removed by horse ambulance to the division hospital about four miles back.

The personnel consisted of 180 *sanitars* or orderlies, three students, and two aids to Kalpaschnecoff.[1] The bulk of the reserve material and the heavy transport wagons, food, feed for horses, etc., were kept at a base situated about three or four miles from the line.

"You will have charge of the advance dressing stations and the main dressing station where operations can be performed," declared the Colonel, "and two of the students will act as your assistants."

Sleeping on the train was almost out of the question, but I suppose we did succeed in getting a cat-nap every now and again despite the poor travelling conditions.

We had breakfast on the train, but in the middle of the day we got off at one of the larger stations for dinner, as there was no provision on the train for regular meals. We rushed into the first-class waiting-room to the buffet where, at a counter, one could purchase zachowsky,[2] similar to our hors-d'oeuvres, various smoked fish, or a dinner of cabbage soup with sour cream, called shee,[3] or cutlets of chopped beef with fried potatoes. Hastily selecting what we desired, we carried it to a table crowded with Russians and disposed of it as quickly as possible.

---

[1] Other accounts include two nurses among the staff of the unit, but Grow does not mention them. See "Young Hero Tells of Russia's 'Flying Column' of Red Cross," *The Nashua Reporter* (Nashua, IA), January 25, 1917, 5.

[2] *Zakuski* (see note 10).

[3] *Shchi*.

The station was packed with a picturesque crowd. There were bearded peasants in dirty sheepskin coats called shubas, with their feet wrapped in cloths over which was fitted a basket work affair made from the bark of trees, fastened to the feet by strings which criss-crossed up the leg to just below the knee, where it was tied and served to hold the cloths in place. This is the usual footwear of the peasant class in the summer or when the weather is dry.

Some, more fortunate, wore leather boots. Soldiers were crowded together, smoking, sleeping on the floor, or talking in little groups, waiting for the train to take them back to the front from their furlough. Most of them were great hulking fellows with bland, childlike faces, mostly blond types with brown-reddish hair and blue eyes, many wearing the orange and black ribbon and little silver cross of the Order of St. George, which is given only for conspicuous bravery under fire.

There were many little family groups in which the women were red-eyed from weeping as a father or son or brother left them to take his place in the train. They were primitive[4] and unashamed in their grief, and as the train pulled out from the station and the loved one swung aboard, their wailing rose above the grind of the car-wheels and the shrieking of the locomotive whistle, the women with aprons covering their faces swaying backward and forward in heart-rending agony.

One little incident at this station made a deep impression upon me. I saw an old, blear-eyed woman, dirty beyond belief, bidding farewell to a fine young fellow who was evidently her son—more than likely her only son. The big fellow kissed her tenderly. He was a fine picture of vigorous manhood as he stood there with his blond head bared while the old mother touched her fingers to his forehead and breast, making the sign of the cross. He stood on the step as the train gathered speed, while the old woman ran stiffly along the tracks in her heavy boots, the tears streaming down her weather-beaten old face calling out her blessing on the departing soldier-boy as she ran.

The country near Petrograd is sparsely settled. Indeed, that huge city with its sparkling golden domes reminds one of a gem set down in the midst of a great green table, for the surrounding country is a flat expanse of green forest.

Now, however, we were reaching a section where more villages were noticeable. They were little gray groups of thatched houses built of logs, huddled together, surrounded by fields of rye and wheat and garden patches. Beyond always stretched the great dark pine forests, the white trunks of the birches showing ghost-like through gloomy cathedral aisles of pines, the sky steel gray and sullen. Over all hung a peculiar sadness, a sullenness of earth and sky, indescribable yet surely there.

What is it that produces the mysterious melancholy of this great country—a mystery and melancholy written deep in the character and in the person of all its

---

[4] The derogatory stereotype of Russians as "primitive" was not uncommon among Westerners at this time.

people? Is it the vast distances, the flatness of the landscape, the lonesomeness of the Northland, the gloom of the forests, the long, cold sunless winters that reflect on the peasant clad in his sheepskin coat, standing there in the field, a little lonesome human atom on the great far stretching expanse of field and forest and swamp? I do not know, but it is there—as mysterious and yet as certain as life itself. One feels it instinctively.

That night we retired early. We were thoroughly tired out from the journey, with its long halts at the stations and the close, stuffy atmosphere of the coach.

The Russian cars, first-class, are fairly comfortable although not very clean. The trains make only about twenty miles per hour on the average, but time is no particular object in Russia and one becomes accustomed to the slowness of travel. The engines burn wood on most lines, huge piles of the fuel racked, split and ready to be thrown into the tender as needed being on hand at the stations.

The next morning, at a station, we had coffee and bread and butter—the customary breakfast in Russia. We had time to take a short stroll on the station platform before the train pulled out. The day was crisp with a touch of autumn and the sun was shining brightly. Most of the passengers were out stretching their legs. I noticed a number of them—soldiers, officers and civilians—running with tea-kettle in hand to a large boiler, and asked the Colonel what they were doing.

"That's just plain water," he explained. "Fire is kept burning under these water boilers, which are called *kipetocks*,[5] day and night, at all stations. No un-boiled water is drunk in Russia. This accounts for the small amount of typhoid in this otherwise unsanitary land."[6]

The soldiers filled their kettles and dashed back to the train, and as we walked through some of the second and third class cars, we saw them bring out little china teapots, cans of tea, sugar, and glasses, and proceed to brew tea which they drank from the glasses.

"Men always drink tea from glasses, women from cups," explained the Colonel. "It is considered effeminate for a man to drink from a cup." At first the absence of ice-water or even cold water was very annoying to me, but I soon became accustomed to tea and before I left Russia I was consuming from ten to fifteen glasses of tea a day and never thought of drinking water.

---

[5] *Kipiatok*.

[6] Typhoid (which is not the same as typhus) is a disease of the gastrointestinal tract caused by impure water and food supplies. The rate of typhoid was actually quite high in the Russian army—with 97,522 soldiers treated between August 1914 and September 1917—and the mortality rate was 21.9%, making it the most common form of infectious disease to affect the Russian troops. See Sanborn, *Imperial Apocalypse*, 162.

The tracks near the station were being repaired and I noticed that the work was done by women.[7] They were mostly young or middle-aged—all great strong creatures with arms and hands and shoulders like men, swinging a pick or shovel or tamping bar without any apparent effort. Although they were bare-footed, they walked about over the rough stone ballast, carrying heavy ties, with apparent unconcern. They were supervised in their labors by a man who leaned indolently against a telegraph pole smoking a cigarette. We noticed many such crews along the line.

Eventually we arrived at Ceslivano, a station about thirty miles from our base. A large sector of the front is supplied from this station. Numerous sidings with cars laden with munitions, huge piles of material under canvas covers, stacks of baled hay as large as houses, and similar stores marked it as an important point. Wagon-loads knee-deep in mud converged to the loading platforms, and hundreds of little two-wheeled carts drawn by a single horse were coming and going, the horse's fetlock deep in sticky brown mud, toiling slowly along over roads which apparently meandered off through fields and forest—diverging like the ribs of a fan over the vast landscape towards the west, where the trenches lie.

We had to transfer our baggage to a little narrow-gauge road which ran to a station a few miles from our base. A toy engine and several flat cars were standing there. Ivan, Kalpaschnecoff's orderly or *deenshick*,[8] who had met us at the station, carried our luggage.

On the way we passed great rows of low buildings which looked like barracks but which were really an immense evacuation hospital.

I was astonished at the terrible condition of the roads. We had to cross one which was a veritable sea of mud, up to our knees. When we reached the other side I noticed an old peasant in the middle of a similar morass of ooze, trying to get to terra firma. He had a bundle in one hand and was holding up his dirty old sheepskin shuba in the other.

Apparently his boots were securely anchored and he couldn't move. He let go his coat and attempted to pull his feet out by lugging at his boot straps. He tugged and tugged and finally lost his balance and to save himself plunged his arm into the mud up to the shoulder. He extricated his arm, righted himself and stood helplessly holding the dripping member out and staring at it as though he didn't recognize it.

Several soldiers saw the old fellow's sad plight and waded out, forming a sort of human chain holding on to each other's hands. The peasant reached out to the one closest to him, they gave a heave and out he came—minus his boots! The old man had no stockings on and he walked off in his bare feet, shaking his head disgustedly.

---

[7] Female labor was essential to the war effort, coming to comprise over 50% of the workforce by 1917, and women were often employed in jobs that were traditionally reserved for men, particularly in Western countries.

[8] *Denshcik*: an officer's personal servant (British batman).

"This is our muddy season," Kalpaschnecoff explained, rather unnecessarily. "In the spring it is somewhat worse. At these times, no army can conduct an offensive in Russia because supplies cannot be brought up quickly enough."

We boarded one of the little flat cars, in company with other officers, and were presently chugging up hill and down dale along hastily laid ties, little grading having been done. Several times, indeed, the rails spread and we ran off the track. Then we would all get off and, by means of crow bars, lift the little cars back and start off again.

I did not know just how close to the front the railroad ran and kept looking at the clear blue sky far away on the horizon for the white puffs of shrapnel which I had heard about; but I saw nothing nor could I even hear the sound of a cannon. After numerous delays, we arrived at our station, a solitary house in the midst of a great dark forest of pines. Here we found a dilapidated victoria[9] drawn by three horses awaiting us.

As Kalpaschnecoff stood talking to the orderly who was in charge of the victoria, I heard a sound like distant thunder muttering on a hot afternoon in summer—far off in the west over the tops of the dark pine trees. Where we stood all was serene and peaceful, but that distant rumbling told me of the grim tragedy that was being enacted along the far borders of that dark forest down whose dismal aisles I vainly peered—gloomy, sunless, mysterious.

"We must be getting on, Grow," declared the Colonel, interrupting my reverie; "it is five miles to our base. Ivan will stay here with the baggage. We will send a wagon for it."

The Colonel and I climbed in the old carriage, and off we went down the muddy road, lurching along, the horses straining at the traces.

As the late autumn twilight fell, we passed a company of sappers returning from a reserve trench-digging operation. They plodded silently by in the gloom, shovels and picks over shoulder, cigarettes glowing, the pungent odor of *Makorka*[10]—the cheap tobacco from the Caucasus which the Russian soldier invariably smokes—permeating the crisp night air.

We passed through a little village. Close to the road were log-houses with projecting thatched eaves and small windows, through which, in the dim candle light, we could see little groups of soldiers sitting around tables drinking tea, and we could hear the sounds of a concertina and a man's voice singing in a high sweet tenor a plaintive Russian romance.

"That's a reserve regiment in billet," the Colonel explained.[11]

---

[9] A low, light, four-wheeled carriage for two with a folding top and a raised driver's seat in front.

[10] *Makhorka*: a coarse tobacco (*Nicotiana rustica*) grown especially in the Ukraine.

[11] It was common practice for soldiers to be billeted in the homes of local villagers.

We gradually ascended to higher ground, passing a column of transport wagons, the drivers of which yelled at their horses as they got mixed up in a bad spot. From the high ground we got a glimpse of black pine tops outlined against a greenish horizon where the sun had set, fading to the dark blue of the upper sky, a crescent moon apparently just balanced on the spire of a distant pine-tree, while far off a white rocket rose gracefully into the air, hung poised a second, and fell from view behind the screening forest. It was a most impressive picture.

"The positions are there," said the Colonel, pointing in the direction of the rocket. "It is about eight miles away. You can see the rockets at intervals all night long. When there is any fighting, the trenches just spout them in a steady stream."

Presently we entered another village and drew up before a house of log and thatch identical to hundreds I had seen.

"Here we are," said the Colonel, as I followed him to the door; "this is our base."[12]

---

[12] Most likely this would have been located north of the Belorussian city of Minsk, on the Russian Western Front, where the 1st Siberian Army Corps was assigned to serve as part of the First Army between August 1915 and February 1916.

Chapter VI

THE SPECTACLE IN THE FROZEN LAKE

We entered a small room, the greater portion of which seemed occupied by a great stove built of stone and mortar, a crude yet efficient affair, with a huge open grate over which could be seen glowing embers, and a great oven above of masonry.

Seated in front of the fire, in the dim light of a tallow candle, was a very old peasant woman, with several dirty children pulling at her dress.

"This house has been commandeered," the Colonel explained to me. "We have taken over the other room and the peasants occupy this one."

I looked around for a bed, but the only furniture was a chair, a rough table, a bench, and the stove.

"You're looking for the bed?" the Colonel asked, sensing my question. "That's on top of the stove. Russian peasants always sleep that way in winter." Sure enough, on top of the masonry oven, just under the low ceiling, was a pile of dirty bedclothes.

"How many live here?" I asked.

"Four. This old woman, the two children—her grandchildren—and their mother."

We passed into the next room. It was larger and lighted by a lamp. A rough pine table with benches around it, and two cots, with a chair or so, comprised the furniture. A young man arose from the table, laying down a book, as we entered. "Metia!"[1] exclaimed the Colonel, addressing him, "I have brought an American doctor to work with you. Now you can improve your English!" Metia was a short, chubby fellow, with a round smiling face, long black hair, greatly disordered, and honest brown eyes, like those of a faithful dog.

He came over smiling and shook hands with me.

"I take great pleasure to see you," he said with a quaint accent.

"Dimitre Paulovitch[2] is one of my best students," said the Colonel. "He was in his third year at the Medical College at Saratoff when war broke out. He has been with me ever since. He will work with you. We call him Metia for short."

Metia then explained that he was in charge of the base for the present and had been going over the medical, surgical, and reserve supplies—taking stock, as it were.

---

[1] Mitia (common nickname for Dmitri).

[2] Dmitri Pavlovich.

The Colonel's aids were away buying forage and supplies. The other two students were in the advance dressing station.

"Everything has been rather quiet," he said. "Not very much work. Just sitting in the trenches—a little sniping and artillery 'straffing' every day to vary the monotony."

He went out to send a wagon for our baggage and to hurry up dinner.

"A great boy that," said the Colonel. "As brave as a lion. He has received the medal of St. George[3] but he never wears it except when he must—when we are inspected or at official dinners. You will find him a great help."

When Metia returned he said that dinner would follow in a few minutes. It consisted of a young sucking pig, brown and crisp, with cassia.[4] Cassia is steamed whole buckwheat, the outer husk being removed, and is one of the staples in Russia, taking the place of potatoes. The soldiers receive it at least once every day.

Then we had *kessil*[5]—a gelatinous substance made from potato flour and water and the extract of a red berry resembling the cranberry. It makes a delicious dessert.

After dinner our baggage came. Ivan made up my cot beside the Colonel's and Metia's and we all turned in.

As I lay there in the darkness, I could hear the occasional low rumble of artillery, which caused the windows of the room to rattle.

The next morning the Colonel announced that we would have to call on the Commander of the Corps.

The old victoria was at the door and we drove off toward the staff, which was located in a big manor house. This house had been deserted by its owners when the tide of battle had ebbed and flowed in this section. A month or two before, the Germans had followed up the Russians in their retreat from Warsaw right to this very locality, but later they had fallen back to their present positions which they had prepared.

We passed two lakes around which desperate hand to hand fighting had taken place only a few weeks previously. The fields and meadows near the lakes were scarred by fresh lines of yellow earth marking hastily constructed trenches, while shell-holes pitted the road on which we were travelling.

The old manor house, a huge white affair of stone and plaster, was situated in a beautiful park. For some reason it had not suffered from artillery fire.

As we drove up to the great door, two sentries with fixed bayonets came to attention. Inside, our coats and hats were taken by an orderly. Another led the way up a broad staircase through a bare hallway, the naked boards resounding under our feet, to a large room with many windows. A log fire was burning in an open fireplace

---

[3] The St. George's Medal and the St. George's Cross were awarded to military personnel who demonstrated bravery and courage in action.

[4] *Kasha.*

[5] *Kissel.*

and the white walls were covered with many-colored maps. A telephone switchboard and telegraph instrument on a table at which sat three operators, gave the room a businesslike appearance.

A tall officer, who had been seated at a table in the center of the room, rose as we entered and greeted us.

Kalpaschnecoff introduced us and asked in Russian to see the Commander of the Corps. The officer sent an orderly for the General, and in the meantime the chief of staff, a short, thick-set man of fifty-five, resplendent with crosses and medals, with a beetling forehead rising dome-like to a perfectly bald head and with a hawk-like nose, came in and was introduced. He spoke a little English and welcomed me quite cordially.

The door opened and General Pleschcoff,[6] commander of the First Siberian Army Corps, entered. Kalpaschnecoff had telegraphed him I was coming and as he advanced his face was wreathed in a smile and his little black eyes twinkled in a most friendly manner.

He embraced Kalpaschnecoff, kissing him on both cheeks in real Russian fashion, and then shook hands with me. He made a cordial little speech in Russian, speaking no English, which the Colonel translated.

"Come, be seated. Have a cigarette? Orderly, the samovar!" he ordered, leading the way to a table and offering his large silver cigarette case covered with many monograms in gold.

He was the most kindly, lovable chap I had met in a long time, and like everyone else, as I found, I soon grew to love him.

Sixty-five years old, with the physique of an athlete, of middle height, stubby thick black hair close cropped, his face seamed and lined by outdoor life, immaculate, erect, vigorous, he made an ideal commander.

After the interview, on the way back to our base, Kalpaschnecoff told me how brilliantly the General had directed his Siberians through the desperate fighting before Warsaw, at Lodz, Prosnitch,[7] and in a dozen other great battles, how he had arrived at Warsaw with troops fresh from the trenches at Galicia and had led them straight from the trains into the midst of the conflict, turning the tide of the second German drive on Warsaw, saving the city and receiving the personal thanks of the Grand Duke Nicholas.

---

[6] General Mikhail M. Pleshkov (1856–1927), a career officer and nobleman who had been commissioned in the Russian Imperial Army since 1894 and served in various cavalry units before being granted command of the 1st Siberian Army Corps. Following the October Revolution in 1917, he fought with the White Guards against the Bolsheviks in the Far East, leading the attempt to recapture Vladivostok. Following the White loss in the Civil War, he emigrated to Harbin, China, where he died.

[7] Przasnysz, a town in Poland approximately 100 km north of Warsaw.

After lunch, Kalpaschnecoff returned to the staff to transact some business, and Metia and I went out for a walk.

He took me to the trench-scarred field between the two lakes we had passed that morning on our way to the staff. Close observation revealed how desperately the opposing armies had battled. The German trenches, hastily dug, without barbed wire, had been badly battered by the Russian artillery; and pieces of clothing, German helmets, discarded gas masks and empty cartridges littered the field where the fighting had occurred only twelve days before.

We walked down to the nearest lake. The trenches ran right to its edge. The bank was steep and overhanging. The last few nights had been cold and a clear sheet of ice covered the lake. Metia slid down the bank to the water's edge and tested the ice gingerly, for the lake was very deep, even close in shore.

I saw him walking carefully out, looking down through the ice, which was like glass, and then suddenly a piercing cry rang out—a cry of intense horror and fright.

I turned quickly, expecting to see Metia struggling in the water, but instead I saw him standing on the ice, his head and body slightly bent forward, his hands clenched. He was looking down into the depths of the lake, his face blanched and an expression of extreme horror depicted on his features.

What terror lurked beneath the surface?

I stumbled down the bank, bringing down a shower of sod and earth, and walked quickly out to where Metia stood transfixed, not more than twelve feet from shore.

"Mister Grow, look! Look!" he cried, as I reached his side.

I looked at the spot he indicated.

Great God! What a visage gazed up at me from under my feet, scarce two inches of crystal ice separating it from the air. I saw a face, bloated, with dull fishy eyes wide open, staring upward, the teeth exposed grinning, the hands like talons apparently trying to push through the glass-like cover of ice. A gray uniform covered the body, which was that of a German.

Nearby, not six feet away, we found a similar horror, but this one had on the brown uniform of Russia.

The two hideous relics in juxtaposition told their own tragic story.

Twelve days before, these two had locked in mortal combat on that overhanging bank. They had stumbled and plunged into the deep icy water of the lake. With deadly persistence they had fought on, down in the deep water, had come up struggling once, twice, perhaps three or four times, only to disappear again—at last, for good! Their fingers had been unlocked from each other's throats only by the great peace-maker—death; and then, in course of time, when nature had by her chemistry of decomposition caused certain gases to form in their carcasses, they had risen from their bed in the eel-grass to the surface, upon which a thin clear covering of ice had formed in the meantime, and there they were with their faces flattened against its restraining surface like those of children against the glass of a window in which is displayed something they yearn for!

Metia quickly recovered his composure and we started silently back towards the village, and then we sent some of our orderlies out with axes and picks and shovels to release the two bodies and bury them on shore.

Chapter VII
THE PROFESSOR OF MATHEMATICS

Early the next morning, Colonel Kalpaschnecoff, Metia and I started out to visit the advanced dressing stations in the trenches.

We rode little Siberian ponies with Cossack saddles. At first, my saddle—a wooden frame with a high back over which a pillow about two inches thick had been strapped—felt rather uncomfortable, but I soon became accustomed to it. Our road led through a great expanse of fields, bare and desolate except for a few carrion crows—big fellows with gray wings and neck and black bodies, which walked stiffly about, their feathers fluffed out against the cold.

We clattered through a little village, the hoofs of our ponies rattling on the frozen ground. There were a few soldiers moving about in the chill morning air, and soldiers' faces peered out at us from the windows of the houses. Then we entered the great dark pine forest through which the road ran some few miles.

"This was the hunting preserve of a very wealthy Polish count," explained the Colonel, pulling his horse up beside mine. "The staff of the regiment and our main dressing station are in the big house in which he lived, which is only a mile from the trenches. It is fairly well screened by the forest but the Germans know its position exactly and they know we are using it, but they have never shelled it. I have an idea that they intend to advance soon and wish to keep the house intact to use themselves. Probably some old German general has his eye on it and is saving it for his own use."

After several miles of forest, we came to a *zemlanka* or dug-out town. Here was billeted a regiment in reserve. The trees were thinned and sufficient were left to screen the "village" from hostile aeroplanes. Little could be seen above ground except mounds of earth partly concealed by pine boughs, and chimneys of mud and stones from which smoke ascended.

It was hard to realize that in that underground community there were living 4,500 men.

"We have not sufficient villages to provide billets for our troops along the Russia front," the Colonel remarked," but our men are able to take care of themselves in the way you see. We just turn them loose in a forest like this, and with picks and shovels and axes they build themselves very comfortable dug-outs in a couple of days."

We dismounted, tied our horses to a tree, and went into one of the earth houses. We had to descend some five or six steps cut in the earth and then entered a door made of saplings nailed together. It was rather dark inside but warm.

As we entered a loud voice called sharply: "*Smeerna!*"[1]—"Attention!"—and twenty men stood erect in the narrow aisle between the bunks on either side.

"*Volna!*"[2]—"At ease!"—ordered the Colonel, and the men relaxed. The Colonel explained that we wished to see their quarters, and they smilingly made way for us.

The Russian soldier always carries with him a roll of rye straw, about two inches thick, six feet long and two and a half wide, held together at the edges by cord woven into the straw. This produces a dry, comfortable pallet which, when unrolled, can be easily dried, or burned when soiled and a new one made, for each man makes his own.

These pallets were thrown on the bunks, which were made of saplings covered with pine boughs. The dug-out was heated by a stove cleverly constructed of brick and mud. As it was below the surface of the ground, the walls were of earth but the roof was of closely laid poles covered by a layer of pine boughs and then a thick layer of earth.

After inspecting the dug-out, we remounted and rode on, coming finally to a large clearing in the center of which stood the great house where the regimental staff was quartered.

As we dismounted, a battery nearby let go four shots in rapid succession, followed by the whiz of the shells as they sped away toward the German lines a mile distant.

I had heard only faint artillery fire that morning—just a distant muttering far to the north and the sudden sharp bark of the battery at close quarters—they were concealed in the woods barely a hundred yards away—startled me and brought home the fact rather suddenly that I was getting near the front.

We first called on the commander of the regiment, a short, bearded man, who was seated at a table in a large room partly dismantled but containing a fine grand piano and several large pieces of old furniture which had apparently proven too heavy to cart off in a hurry.

Colonel Starik greeted me cordially and said he was glad I was to work in his regiment.

We then visited our main dressing station located in what had been the lodge of the gamekeeper.

The student who was to work with me was a little chap, thin, wearing thick spectacles. He had a large generous smile.

He did not speak English but requested Colonel Kalpaschnecoff to ask me to look at a German who had been wounded in "No Man's Land" two nights before and who

---

[1] *Smirno.*

[2] *Vol'no.*

had been found early that morning by a Russian patrol lying half-dead from exposure and brought in.

We entered a little room and as I opened the door my nostrils were assailed by an odor I knew only too well—the unmistakable sign of that dread condition known as gangrenous emphysema.

The wounded German was a fine-looking man of about thirty-six. His great brown eyes looked into mine with the expression of a hunted animal. He was pallid and weak.

I examined the wound. A rifle bullet had entered the thigh near the hip joint and emerged in the groin. The limb was badly discolored and swollen—the purplish area extending up into the abdominal wall. When pressed on, the tissues gave forth a crackling sound caused by minute accumulations of gas produced by the deadly *bacillus*. I turned to the student and he, seeing my expression, led me from the room. I told him, through Metia, that the condition had extended too high in the abdomen for amputation. All we could do was to incise the tissues with long free incisions, drain off the horrid brown discharge and gas, and apply a moist dressing of hydrogen peroxide, which was the treatment then in use in France. "There isn't a chance for him, however," I told Metia, "and you had better talk to him and find out where he lived, who he is, and whether we can do anything for him. He looks very refined—too intelligent for a private."

Metia spoke German well and questioned the German.

In a faint voice, he told us that he was German professor of mathematics in a little college town in Germany, was married and had three children. He had been drafted as a private and was about to be made a sergeant when he was wounded.

"I was ordered by my commanding officer the other night," he said, "to crawl out between the lines and approach the Russian trenches as closely as possible, where I was to listen for a suspected digging party which he feared were running out a sap to lay a mine under our trenches.

"I crawled up close to the Russian barbed wire, and lay there listening. Just after a rocket had flared up from your trenches, several shots were fired and I felt a sharp burning pain in my hip. I tried to move my leg but I couldn't.

"I was bleeding badly and lay a long time waiting for death. I don't know how long. Finally the pain became worse and by a frantic effort I managed to crawl a few yards back toward our lines. My leg dragged on the ground and I crawled with my arms alone, a few feet at a time. It began to grow light in the east. I was so cold, so tired, in so much agony, that when I came to a shell-hole I crawled into it and fainted away. I regained consciousness several times that day and the next night, then I knew nothing until I woke up here. Do you think I will get well? I want to write to my wife. Can a letter be sent from here?"

All this Metia got from him by patient questioning, as he was too weak to talk much at a time. Metia promised to write a letter at his dictation after he had been fixed up a little by the American doctor he had just seen.

He consented to the treatment I had suggested, so we got things ready, gave him some ether and operated.

He reacted fairly well and that evening was able to dictate a pathetic letter to his wife and little ones. He told them that he would be well soon and that while he would be in prison in Russia he did not mind that, as the Russians were good and kind to him. He would not be killed in battle anyway, and was sure to see them again after the war, which could not last much longer. He added that he felt sure of recovering because of the skill of an American surgeon who was attending him.

The poor fellow lived two days. We kept him fairly comfortable with morphine, but the infection was too virulent and he succumbed. They buried him in the little cemetery, under the dark pines, a Russian priest officiating. All the staff attended and we stood with heads bared, while the cold wind sighed through the branches of the trees. A cross of wood with his name and regiment inscribed on it was placed at his grave, where he sleeps in company with others who were once his foes. Metia wrote a second letter to the wife in the little town in Germany.

The kindness which the Russian officers showed to this German during his last few days is worth recording because it is typical of the conduct of the Russian military throughout this whole war—at least for all I was ever able to observe to the contrary. The colonel commanding the regiment came to see the wounded German twice a day to inquire if there was anything he wished, and many other officers would make similar visits every day. But to return to my visit to the regimental staff.

The operation had kept me busy all the afternoon and we did not have time that day to go to the trenches where the two advanced dressing stations were.

After dinner at the staff, an old artillery officer, a colonel, long in the service, sat down at the piano and played some wonderful music, while the rest of us sat about smoking.

Occasionally the windows would rattle and the old house vibrate as a battery nearby would send an evening message to the Germans, but the sound was more or less muffled by the thick walls.

It was difficult to realize that within a mile lay the trenches filled with men striving to kill each other while we sat there listening to the sweet music of Mendelssohn and Rubinstein.

Before retiring I walked out in front of the house. It was dark and still—not a breath of air stirring. Myriads of stars were sparkling coldly in the velvet pall of the heavens. Over the black tops of the pine forests, far away, toward the trenches, the sky suddenly lighted up with a ghostly quivering white glare as a trench rocket split the darkness, flickered a moment, and was gone. Then came the crackle of rifle shots, faint and far off, and then silence again.

I stood listening and watching for more rockets but none appeared and I turned to go in when suddenly the air was filled with a horrid screeching sound. Nearer and nearer it came from the black sky overhead, over the pines, increasing in intensity as it approached and its pitch growing shriller. I instinctively crouched, my muscles tense, my teeth clenched, waiting I knew not for what. Whatever it was seemed to be about to land at my feet. Then came a red angry flash, followed by a terrific explosion, in the forest a hundred yards to my right, and a humming in the air like the sound a large nail used to make when I had thrown it as a child, and then the sound of falling fragments of earth and metal. A horse screamed over where the thing had burst.

Kalpaschnecoff had strolled calmly out to where I stood, his cigarette glowing in the darkness.

"The Boches[3] are straffing our battery a bit," he said. "Here comes another!"

Sure enough I could hear the same screaming sound as the big shell described its trajectory, then another flash and roar in the trees and the humming of steel fragments in the air.

This time I did not mind it so much. With the Colonel by my side, it was not so lonely, and I had a warning of what was coming.

"Will our battery answer?" I asked.

"Not now; they are sitting down snugly in their bomb-proofs. What would be the use of their exposing themselves? You say you heard a horse scream? Likely they are bringing up ammunition and one of the cannon team was hit. They have cut him loose and driven off by this time, though, and the Germans won't catch another."

The Boches fired only those two shots. Evidently they had hoped to catch some one above ground or a supply column at work unloading shells, and the next morning we learned that the Colonel had been correct in his surmise—one of the lead horses of a caisson[4] which was unloading shells had been hit by a fragment and died in a few moments, but the soldiers had hastily cut the traces and driven off before the second shell had landed.

---

[3] An offensive slang term for Germans, derived from French *alboche*, a combination of the word for "German," *al(lemand)*, and "blockhead," *(ca)boche*.

[4] A usually two-wheeled vehicle for artillery ammunition attachable to a horse-drawn cart.

Chapter VIII
IN THE RUSSIAN TRENCHES

That night we slept on the floor in one of the rooms of the manor house, rolled up in blankets borrowed from officers of the staff, in front of a great log fire.

The next morning a soldier came and inquired for me. He was shown in and said he had been sent to me by the commander of the 8th Regiment by order of General Pleschcoff. He was to be my orderly, having been picked out of 50,000 men in the corps because he spoke English. He had lived two years in America, where he had worked in a Pittsburgh machine-shop. He had earned enough to return home, some six years before the war, and buy a little farm in the province of Omsk, eight hundred miles north of the Trans-Siberian Railroad. He was married and had two children. When war broke out he had been called to the colors, being a reservist, thirty-six years old. He had been in the war since September, 1914, and had not been home in the meantime.

Mike remained my orderly until I left the army and I grew greatly attached to him. Of the great service he rendered me at the risk of his own life I shall write later.

We started off for the trenches, riding part of the way, for the road was well screened by the forest.

We passed the battery which had been fired on the previous evening and stopped a moment to look at the two big shell-holes. They were from twelve to fifteen feet across and about four feet deep. A soldier of the battery was cutting some kindling wood with his *kinjal* or curved dagger, which all the artillery men carry—a heavy knife with a wicked curved blade about two feet long. The trees roundabout were torn and splintered, one, about ten inches in diameter, having been completely severed by a jagged cut.

A few yards off, lying on its side, its feet sticking up stiffly in the air, was a dead horse. I don't know why, but horses always seem to lie that way when killed. The soldier came over when he saw us looking at the horse and explained that it had been killed by the first shell of the night before but that none of the men were hurt.

The guns of the battery were cleverly concealed in pits with a roof of saplings and sod covered with pine boughs. The shells were stored between each gun in very deep bomb-proof shelters with great logs in the roof. There were apparently about six layers of logs and dirt. Eighteen steps led down to the entrance of these little storehouses.

In back of the guns was a deep trench leading to some strongly built bomb-proof shelters where the men and officers lived. By means of this trench, they could approach the guns when being shelled without getting hurt. In back of the trench was the fire control, a heavy bomb-proof affair, with a telephone connecting with the observation point far out in the advanced trenches in a particularly high spot or even in a tree top. Here the observing officer sits and watches the shells hit, makes the necessary corrections on the range and telephones back to the battery fire control each time he desires it changed. The gunners scarcely ever see their objective or even the explosion of their shells. These particular guns were firing over a forest at least three-quarters of a mile wide.

"We are just beginning to get shells," remarked the Colonel. "Those villainous traitors in Petrograd, bought by the Germans, had the factory near Moscow working for nearly six months on shells just a little too large to go into our guns. The blue print patterns were a fraction of a millimeter off—just enough to make the shells useless. I refer to the Ministers of War and Munitions and their hirelings—especially that dastard Sukhomlinoff!"

"Ah! Russia Russia! poor Russia!" sighed Metia. "Here we had those fine little guns, so quick, twenty shots a minute, and no shells! and the German artillery—oh!" and he waved his arms and rolled his eyes, unable to express his disgust.

We remounted and rode on for half a mile through beautiful pines to a bend in the road where we dismounted, tied our horses to trees, and proceeded on foot.

The occasional crack of a rifle rang out in the crisp air, only now and then, not often. It reminded me of the first day of the deer season in the northwoods at home—the cold, clear air, the odor of pines, and the occasional echoing reports, some far off, some near.

The trees were thinning now and the light of an open space shone through ahead.

We entered an approach trench, which extended forward in a zigzag. It was not very deep and the Colonel said: "Keep your head down at the turns or you may be seen by a sniper!"

We paused for a moment at a support trench built about 300 feet back of the first line trench. Rows of barbed-wire, criss-crossed from poles about four feet high driven in the ground, were in front of it.

"Here is our dressing-station," announced the Colonel, as he led the way to the entrance of a dug-out built in the wall of the trench.

We descended some eight or ten steps. The roof was of logs and dirt. The door was a regular door evidently taken off some partly destroyed house. Inside it was dark at first, but as my eyes became accustomed to the gloom, I saw I was in a little room about eight feet wide by fifteen feet long. A small stove of brick and stone occupied one end. At the other was a crude table on which were bandages and instruments covered by a white cloth. A stretcher served as an operating table, resting on four stakes driven in the earth floor, a candle stuck in the neck of a bottle serving for light. There were several benches, and near the stove a cot from which rose a very dishevelled youth.

Kalpaschnecoff introduced him as Nicholi Alexandrovitch. He was one of the students. He was a tall, gangling fellow, with a large head, slightly stooping shoulders, and a lean neck which did not seem strong enough to support the massive cranium.

"*Skuchna esdes*—it is tiresome here," he said. "No work—only three wounded yesterday. We have another station like this a quarter of a mile to the right. You will visit both every day and also the main station back at the big house. I will have your stuff sent out today from the base. You can live here or at the main station, as you wish. It is more comfortable back there, however."

"Thanks," I replied; "I will have my things brought here. There is room for another cot and I want to learn this trench-life and live it also, and, if you don't mind, I'll stay right here."

"As you wish," said the Colonel.

"Meester is not afraid of the German *granata* (shells)," said Metia.

"Yes, I am; very much afraid," I admitted. "That's why I'm staying. I want to get used to them."

We all walked down the approach-trench to the fire-trench.

"Keep very quiet here," warned the Colonel. "The German trenches are only seventy-five meters distant and they always listen for any noise or movement in our trenches. If they hear anything they send over a grenade from a trench mortar or some shells from the artillery, hoping to catch some one exposed."

Spee! A ricochet sang over our heads and I ducked as it passed by. It had such a nasty sound I could not help dodging, and I felt like a fool afterwards, resolving not to move a muscle the next time.

Bang! crashed a rifle, right at my elbow around the corner of the parapet as we slipped into a fire trench. Again I ducked involuntarily, and resolved again to control my jerky nerves.

As I walked on I felt uncomfortably tall and was sure the top of my head was above the trench. I was surprised at the small number of men on duty—just one to each sector. The trenches are not dug in a straight line but are like the design we used to call the "walls of Troy," the interposed squares of earth limiting the explosive and killing effects of a shell to the particular section in which it falls. If the trenches were straight, a direct hit—that is, a shell falling in the trench—would kill and wound men a hundred yards up and down the trench. There were about eight loopholes to each sector of the fire-trench, then a square-cut elbow around a solid block of earth about eight feet across, called a traverse, then another loopholed sector, and so on.

The Russian trenches have a head cover of timber and dirt as protection against shrapnel. They don't use many sand-bags for loopholing but make a pyramidal shaped box of wood about three feet long, open at both ends, with a 6-inch square opening at the small end and a 2 1/2 feet by 6-inch opening at the large end. This is laid on the earth, large end toward the trench, and then it is covered with dirt and the head cover constructed. This gives a loophole with plenty of elbow-room to move a rise about, a good place to rest it on, and a 6-inch opening at the far end to stick the end of the gun through. A fire-step is made on the side of the trench on which the soldier stands while firing and which brings his face level with the loophole.

You feel quite lonely and isolated when in one of these little sectors of fire-trench. This day there was only one soldier to a sector although not eighty yards away was an enemy anxious to attack. It seemed as if all they had to do was to walk over and take us all prisoners.

Then I noticed the funk-holes, as they are called on the English front. They are small excavated rooms in the side of the trench, in each of which were crowded eight or ten soldiers lying about, sleeping, smoking, or talking in low tones. In many, through the open passage-way could be seen charcoal braziers filled with glowing embers—the braziers consisting of buckets, powder-cans or large meat tins in which holes had been punched.

We stopped at one of the empty loopholes and peered out over the barbed wire across No Man's Land toward the German trenches. All I could see of the German positions was a haze of tangled wire and crooked stakes and a ridge of earth which was sod-covered in some places and bare in others. Although the German trenches were only about seventy-five yards away, no loopholes could be seen and there was not a sign of life nor a moving thing. It looked for all the world like a field in which great ground moles had been digging and tunneling and, growing tired of their labors, had wandered off.

The opposing lines faced each other across a shallow ravine, ours right on the edge of the forest. The Germans had about three hundred yards of open field in back of their first line, then a dense forest—black and mysterious.

The striking thing to me was the entire absence of anything to shoot at, and yet snipers were constantly at work in our trenches and every minute or two a shot would ring out. The Germans were equally active and the crack of their bullets as they landed in the trees and the spee of their ricochets were frequently heard. The trees were simply torn to pieces by shells and bullets and presented a very bedraggled and skeleton-like appearance.

Kalpaschnecoff walked up to a little soldier who was gazing intently out of his loophole, firing away at something every couple of minutes. Scattered about his feet was a considerable pile of empty brass cartridges.

"Well, Galoopchick[1] (little dove)"—they always call the soldiers and peasants that—"Galoopchick, what are you firing at?"

---

[1] *Golubchik*: term of endearment. Literally "little dove," but colloquially like "dear," "deary," or "honey."

"Your Excellency, I have been at this loophole several hours every day for eight days," the little dove, who was certainly a very much soiled little dove, his face blackened from the smoke and coal of a brazier, replied. "Every few minutes, all the time I am here, a German over there waves a white flag. I shoot every time he waves that flag and still he waves it. Look now! Your Excellency will see it there—right along the top of my rifle barrel. I have pointed it right at the white flag!"

Kalpaschnecoff looked, squinting along the barrel of the rifle. Then he pulled out a pair of field binoculars and gazed long and hard. Finally he turned to me and handed me the glasses. I looked, and sure enough something white was moving; it moved to and fro for a minute and then stopped. "Looks to me like a piece of old paper partly buried in the parapet of their trenches," I said.

"I think you are right," the Colonel agreed; and then turning to the soldier: "There, little dove, you are a faithful one to fire so often and carefully at what you thought was a German waving a flag, but it isn't a flag; it's a paper moving in the wind. Don't bother about it!"

The little fellow looked unconvinced as we moved on but, of course, he obeyed orders. "They are like children,"[2] the Colonel commented. "As a matter of fact, though, a man standing for hours gazing at one object can hypnotize himself into believing almost anything. This trench warfare produces some funny nerve conditions. That soldier probably thinks the Germans are as tired of fighting as he is and are waving flags of truce. There's an observation point on that knoll," pointing to a rise of ground ahead; "we'll go and have a look."

The trench sloped gently upward and presently we came to a strongly built bomb-proof on the very highest part. All the trees had been torn down by shell-fire and the top of the little hill was torn and scarred. Two periscopes peeped up through holes in the thick roof of the dug-out. An officer was sitting at one, his eye glued to the eye-piece, slowly turning the milled screw-head which turned the periscope and changed its visual field.

"Be in good health, Lieutenant!" the Colonel greeted.

"Hello, Andrea Ivanovitch!"[3] he replied. "What brings you here?"

The Colonel explained that he was showing me around, and introduced me to Lieut. Muhanoff.

The Lieutenant was a man of thirty-six but looked older. His face was covered with a scraggly brown beard and his near-sighted, humorous eyes peered through gold-rimmed spectacles. He looked more like a good-natured schoolmaster than a soldier.

---

[2] A commonly-held conception among the Russian officer corps, who, at least in the initial years of the war, were comprised of those from the upper classes of society, and tended to view the peasant-soldiers in a highly patronizing way.

[3] Andrei Ivanovich.

"He speaks English," said Kalpaschnecoff, "but he's bashful and pretends he doesn't. Come on now, show the American how well you do!"

"I speak a very, very little—very badly. I have been to your America. Two months I was there. Yes, San Francisco, New York—ah, New York! I thought I should go mad—so much noise and confusion. I was glad to get back to dear Russia!" and he smiled apologetically.

"You do very well indeed," I replied, "and you must come to see me. I will be living in the dressing-station and will be glad to talk to someone who has been in America."

"I am commanding the scouts, doing work in No Man's Land," he declared. "I am busy every night but when I have time I will come."

I told him I should like to go with him on some of his expeditions, and he promised to take me. "It is very dangerous, however," he added, "out there between the lines."

That was the beginning of a friendship which lasted almost a year—until one terrible day in September, 1916, when he was killed.

"I am about to have the artillery destroy that old brick building near the German lines. My scouts think they are using it as an observation point. The chimney is still standing and it is quite high. Take a look!" Muhanoff invited.

I looked through the periscope. The trench lines were farther apart here, possibly three hundred yards separating them. In front of the German position, partly demolished, was an old brick building, the chimney towering above the ruined walls.

Muhanoff turned to an artillery officer, who was poring over a map under a celluloid cover with lines marking it off into squares.

"All ready, Lieutenant," he said to the officer. "All ready, sir," the artillery-man repeated, and then he called off a couple of numbers to a soldier seated at a field telephone which communicated with the battery.

The soldier repeated the numbers.

"Now watch through the periscope," said the Lieutenant, addressing me.

I turned the instrument to the building and waited. A minute, maybe two, passed; then a whistling sound in the air overhead and a fountain of dirt and yellow, brown and white smoke shot up just in front of the building, a few yards from the wall, as the high explosive shell struck with a loud crash.

The artillery-man was watching through another periscope. He turned to the soldier and called off several more numbers. They were repeated over the telephone and after another brief wait another shot was fired. This time it scored a perfect hit and a large portion of the wall crumbled down and a shower of bricks, mortar and smoke spurted up.

As I looked I saw through the settling haze of dust a movement as of the glint of sunshine on some bright metal. The artillery-man saw it too, for I heard him sharply cry: "Shrapnel!" and rattle off some more figures hurriedly.

"That last one brought them out!" he cried excitedly, his eyes gleaming. "They have an approach-trench running from their fire-trench out to those ruins. They are crawling back to their trench through it. They didn't stoop enough in their hurry and I saw them move. Quick now with the battery and we'll catch them!" he muttered to himself.

Another screeching and a white cotton-like puff of smoke appeared a hundred feet over the ruins and exploded with a sharp barking report, and the shrapnel scattered its 180 bullets on the ground between the ruins and the German trenches searching out those scurrying Boches running for their lives. Whether any of them were hit, it was, of course, impossible for us to tell.

He continued pounding away at the old building with high explosives until the chimney and walls were all flattened out and nothing remained but a heap of bricks.

"I wonder if that shrapnel caught them in time?" he murmured as he folded up his map, lit a cigarette, and walked out.

As we were going back up the trench toward the dressing station, we turned a corner into a traverse at a point where the lines approach each other closely.

"Look out!" yelled the Colonel, dodging back against the wall of the trench and crouching there. As I scrambled back I caught a glimpse out of the corner of my eye of an oblong object hurtling down into the trench, turning end over end, from the direction of the German lines.

A terrific explosion occurred in the fire sector we were just about to enter. A mass of earth and wood flew up high in the air and showered down on us, covering us with dirt.

"A big grenade from a trench mortar," said the Colonel, brushing himself off. "Fortunately they come slow enough to be seen in the daytime."

The block of earth separating the two fire sectors had protected us, but the poor fellow at watch in the next sector had not fared so fortunately. We found him badly mangled, half buried in earth and timber from the caved-in parapet. He was still breathing as I stooped over him, but died before we could get him out from under the debris which was piled on his lower extremities. His head had been crushed like an eggshell by a huge fragment of the grenade.

Several more were fired at our trench a hundred yards lower down, but did no damage, as they were not direct hits.

The soldiers in the funk-holes[4] nearby crawled out and picked up their fallen comrade by the feet and arms and carried him off to an approach trench, his head hanging back and bumping on the uneven ground. Another posted himself at a loop-hole which had not been destroyed by the grenade. Others started to patch up the parapet under the direction of an officer. There was no excitement. It was all taken as a matter of course. In a few minutes everything was as before in that sector except

---

[4] Small areas scraped out on the side of trenches where soldiers would often sleep.

for a hole in the trench parapet, a few dark stains on the earth, and a different soldier staring out across No Man's Land.

We went back to our dressing station. As we entered the approach-trench we had to step over a huddled object covered with a torn brown overcoat and we met two of our stretcher-bearers approaching with a rolled-up stretcher. Tomorrow a new wooden cross would appear back in the forest taking its place among thousands of others already there.

At the dressing station we found that an orderly had just brought in our dinner. It was carried in porcelain dishes racked or nested together one above the other and held by a wire. It was quite hot and consisted of hot cabbage soup, cutlets of chopped beef, fried potatoes and stewed dried fruit.[5] Tea was made in a little samovar which Nicholi Alexandrovitch always kept with him even here in the trenches.

We seated ourselves on blocks of wood and crude benches, using the stretcher for a table. It was covered with a clean muslin cloth, which I was glad of, as I had noticed several suspicious brownish-red stains on the canvas earlier in the day. We ate from tin plates and had real knives and forks and glass tumblers for our tea.

The soldiers have a tin cup, a small copper pail holding about a quart for their soup, and a large wooden spoon which they carry stuck in their boot leg. The bucket and cup are attached to their belt on the march.

Mike, my new orderly, arrived late in the afternoon with my cot and luggage. The Colonel, Metia and Lieutenant Muhanoff left, and I was alone with Nicholi Alexandrovitch, who could speak no English. I had been plugging away steadily with my Russian and could understand an ordinary conversation but spoke with difficulty. However, we got along fairly well, using Mike when we got into difficulty or resorting to the sign language.

It was snug that night down there in the dug-out. The occasional sound of artillery was muffled by the thick walls.

About eleven o'clock, Nicholi prepared to retire. He stood a long time with the covers of his cot turned down leaning over with a candle in his hand. Long and intently he scrutinized it, the ritual lasting for about ten minutes, and then he blew out the candle and crawled into bed. I supposed it some strange Russian religious ceremony and made no comment.

After a while I too turned in. It was quiet and dark in the dug-out and I soon became drowsy. Just as I was falling asleep, I felt an itchy spot just below the knee. I rubbed it with the other leg and at once developed a similar condition on the ankle of that leg. I concluded that I had eaten something that day which had given me hives. Another and another place started, until I seemed to have half a hundred of them,

---

[5] This simple meal was much better fare than that which rank-and-file soldiers and medical workers would have been given, which often consisted of little more than *sukharki* (dried crusts of black bread), thin soup or kasha, and tea. Officers' food was considerably higher in quantity and quality.

and as I squirmed and tossed about I figured that I must be spotted like a leopard and I got out of bed to see.

I got a candle and lighted it and an examination of my body revealed a typical attack of hives—a very nasty one.

A chuckle, somewhat muffled by the bedclothes, sounded from the student's end of the room.

"*Blockie*,[6] Meester?" inquired a sleepy voice. "No, hives—urticaria," I replied, giving the medical name.

"No, no, Meester; *blockie!*" insisted the student.

"What in the devil are *blockie!*" I asked.

"I will show you," and he shuffled over to my cot, took the candle and searched in my bed. Presently he made a dive at something and presented me with a tiny black mite held between his forefinger and thumb—a little flea.

His strange maneuver before retiring was no longer a mystery to me—it was one I performed or Mike performed for me every night for the next eighteen months!

Nicholi produced some powder from his cot and dusted it over my bed and between the covers, after searching around and finding three more fleas.

"Now, Meester can sleep," he said; and I did very well.

A great blessing is good insect powder on the Russian front!

---

[6] *Blokhi*: fleas. In actuality, these were most likely lice, which infested the trenches of most troops (over 90%) during the Great War.

Chapter IX
I GO "OVER THE TOP"

Next morning, while we were having our tea piping hot from Nicholi's samovar, the stretcher-bearers brought in a badly wounded soldier.

He was covered with a blanket and as they placed him on the stretcher I was amazed at his strange appearance. He was no longer than a child and yet his arms were of the average length and his shoulders were broad.

As he lay under the blood-soaked blanket, he moaned feebly. His face was ghastly, a peculiar greenish white.

As an orderly lifted the blanket, the poor fellow cried out:

"My feet! My feet! My God, don't touch my feet!"

I gazed horror-stricken as the blanket was removed and I saw why he had looked so small. There were no feet! Neither were there any legs to speak of—just stumps bound in blood soaked bandages.

"A high explosive shell dropped in the trench near him and exploded," one of the orderlies, with blanched face, explained to me in a whisper. "A large fragment struck him between the knee and the hip, carrying away both legs. One leg hung by a small strip of skin, Excellency, but I cut it off with my knife, for it was difficult to carry him with it swinging about before we got him on the stretcher."

The orderlies had applied tourniquets, partially checking the hemorrhage.

"Oh! my feet, why do they pain so? Please don't touch them, don't touch them!"[1] he pleaded. I gave him a hypodermic of morphine for the pain and a pint of hot salt solution in one of the veins of his arm, for he had lost much blood.

I tied off the arteries and veins with cat-gut to prevent further hemorrhage and then took off the tourniquets. I then cleaned up the stumps as well as I could, applied iodine to the raw surfaces and put on clean bandages, during all of which he complained bitterly of the pain in his feet—a phenomenon due, of course, to the fact that the nerves which had been severed by the amputation were conveying an erroneous message to the poor fellow's brain.

When he had reacted sufficiently, we placed him in one of our little horse ambulances, which were kept hidden in the forest a few hundred yards back of the trenches,

---

[1] This phenomenon is referred to as "phantom limb pain," which approximately 60–80% of individuals who lose limbs experience.

and started him on his journey to the division hospital, which was located some four miles farther back. As the ambulance slowly rattled off over the rough frozen road, the poor fellow was still crying: "My feet! My feet! How they pain!"

That afternoon, as Nicholi and I were having tea in our dug-out, the door opened and Lieutenant Muhanoff entered. He brushed the powdery snow from his sheepskin coat and walked over to the stove to warm his hands. It was only three-thirty o'clock in the afternoon but already the short Russian day was drawing to a close and we had a candle lighted in the dug-out.

"It will be a thick night—four inches of snow have fallen already," he said. "It will be a fine dark night for the little affair we've planned!"

"What little affair?" I asked.

"Well, we're going to give the Germans a raiding party. It won't amount to much—just two companies—about four hundred men—will go over. The artillery will put up a barrage on their communication trenches and on a certain sector of their first-line trenches which form a salient. An intense fire will be concentrated at the same time on the barbed wire at certain points. This preparation will last about an hour, and then, when the fire on the wire and the first-line lifts, we will go over and our artillery will then fire on the communication trenches and the German batteries to prevent the Germans from escaping and their artillery from putting up a barrage on us."

I showed him that I was very much interested in the modus operandi and he gave me further details.

"We'll only remain in the German trenches about five minutes, but we hope to take some prisoners and possibly some machine guns. The main object, I understand, is to prevent the Germans from sending troops north to the Riga-Dvinsk front where there is some heavy fighting. If you worry them by raids at various points on the line they become nervous, fearing larger attacks, and they won't weaken their line by transferring troops to the region where they are really needed."

The Lieutenant explained the proposed plan to me as simply as possible, aware that I knew nothing of the technical end of the game. He drew a rough map to show the salient we were to attack and the communication trenches where they hoped to cut the Germans off if they attempted to escape.

"I should like very much to go over with you," I said, hardly hoping that I would be allowed to do so.

"You may if you want to," he replied; "but you must remember that it is very dangerous work. We will take stretcher-bearers with us to bring the wounded back and, if you want to, you may go with them. Have you a white operating gown?"

I reached for my gown which was hanging on a hook.

"That's very good. We're all going to wear white on account of the snow. It will make us invisible to the German machine gun and rifle men. Put a pillow-case over your head and you'll do fine!"

I snatched a pillow-case from the cot and put it on.

"You look like a cowled monk," Muhanoff commented; but it will serve first-rate. I will call for you at eight-twenty. We'll go into the first line at that time and watch the artillery preparations, which starts at eight forty-five, and at nine forty-five we will attack. Have you a good revolver? All right, be prepared at eight-twenty!"

He closed the door and was gone.

It was very still there in the dug-out. Nicholi had gone out immediately after tea to visit the other dressing-station and I was all alone. The candle cast flickering shadows on the earthen wall. A coal popped in the stove and it sounded to me like a rifle-shot![2]

A dug-out with good thick walls and a tightly closed door is a very dismal sort of place—more like a tomb than anything else, with the smell of fresh earth and the dampness. It is especially so when you're alone. I felt like a child when left alone in the dark.

It occurred to me that I was doing a very foolish thing—sticking my nose into a dangerous proposition like this which really didn't concern me in the least. A little cold shiver ran up and down my spine. I wondered if the revolver which Dr. Egbert had given me really was all right. I hadn't tried it out and possibly the blamed thing wouldn't work at all or the cartridges were stale or the firing pin gummed up or something. I took it down and examined it and as I opened it up my hand shook. I was frankly in a blue funk!

I looked at my wrist-watch—6:34—three hours and eleven minutes to go! I opened the door and let in an icy blast and a flying swirl of snow.

"What is the matter! Is Meester so warm he keeps the door open?" exclaimed Nicholi, stepping in the open door a moment later, a look of astonishment on his red frosty face at the pile of snow which had blown in and the frigid temperature of the dug-out.

"Oh, no," I replied; "I just wanted to give it a little airing. You can close it now; it is a bit chilly!"

A great deal might happen in three hours and eight minutes. The general might call the little party off or I might stumble in the trench in the dark and break a leg. One can never tell. The reflection made me feel a little better.

The orderly brought our dinner and after dinner we had tea. I drank five or six glasses, and my spirits were considerably brightened. I was in for it now and there was nothing to do but to go through with it.

---

[2] War and the horrors associated with it often had the effect of transforming mundane and innocuous sounds into strange and menacing ones for both soldiers and medical workers. See Laurie Stoff, "The Sounds, Odors, and Textures of Russian Wartime Nursing," in *Russian History through the Senses: From 1700 to the Present*, ed. Tricia Starks and Matthew Romaniello (New York: Bloomsbury Academic Publishing, 2016), 117–40.

I GO "OVER THE TOP"

Promptly at eight-twenty, Lieutenant Muhanoff came in, his scraggly beard plastered with snow and ice. He stood by the stove combing it out with his fingers. He looked like a bespectacled, bearded imitation of a stage ghost, with his white gown and peeked head covering.

In his hand he held two peculiar objects which looked like tomato cans with long handles on them, and there were two more in his belt, which he wore outside his white coat.

"They are hand grenades," he explained, observing me looking at them. "They are very useful to have at times, especially if you are not a dead shot with a revolver. One of these things will usually get anything within a radius of five meters when it explodes. You had better take these two with you."

He showed me how to insert the capsule, as he called it, and how to throw it, retaining in my hand the little metal ring which fitted over the handle.

"When you throw it, hold on to the ring and let the bomb go, slipping the ring off the handle," he said. "This releases the spring which starts the time fuse. The time fuse burns four seconds after the ring is pulled off and then the bomb explodes. It is well to drop flat on the ground when you throw it, especially if it does not fall in a trench—you'll be less apt to be hit by fragments." I took one of the things gingerly in my hand. "Any danger of it going off from a jar?" I asked.

"No, not unless you knock the ring off."

I determined to be very gentle and to keep my hand on those rings in going over the rough spots. "You can carry a bomb in your right hand and your revolver in your left," said the Lieutenant, as I put on my white coat and the pillow-slip over my head. He strapped the other bomb in its sling on my belt outside the coat. As we started out, Nicholi solemnly shook hands with both of us, wishing us good luck.

As I stepped out of the door, I thought hell had been turned loose.

The air was full of a variety of sounds running the scale from a screech to the noise an express train makes when going over a trestle while you are standing underneath.

"The high-pitched scream is from the three inch shells, and the deep roar is from the six-inch howitzer[3] shells," the Lieutenant shouted in my ear. "Hurry! This way!" he said, slipping quickly down an approach-trench. "The Boches will start to reply in a minute and we must get under cover!"

The roar of the artillery was terrific.

Through the tree-trunks ahead and in the sky above their black tops, I could see the flickering white flare of a steady stream of rockets from the German trenches.

"We've got them throwing up their fire-works!" the Lieutenant shouted as we stumbled on.

---

[3] A type of artillery piece with a short barrel and which uses comparatively small charges to propel projectiles over relatively high trajectories, with a steep angle of descent.

It was snowing thickly and the flickering rockets produced peculiar diffused light effects, indistinct yet very powerful.

In the first line, we joined hundreds of other white ghosts. Some had glowing cigarettes in their mouths, and the pungent smell of *makorka*, the vile tobacco they smoke, was in the air.

They stood about, leaning against the trench parapet, talking in subdued voices in little groups. Some sat on the fire-step alone and silent with white sheeted head bowed, waiting for the signal to go over the top. A very few were laughing and joking, but it was nervous laughter and some peered intently out over No Man's Land through the loopholes. Those who were not going to take part in the raid but were to remain in the trenches acting as reserves did not have on the white coats.

"Come here and look through the loophole!" said the Lieutenant in my ear.

As I started toward him I heard shells which had a different sound from ours—a sound which rose gradually in pitch as though near the end of a song. They were German shells. It was their reply to our bombardment and several times I saw a red flash through the loophole, accompanied by a close stunning explosion which sounded as if limbs of trees and things were falling around us.

At the culmination of a particularly vicious whiz, a terrific crash with a red flash of light occurred about sixty feet down the trench, apparently right on the parapet. The ground shook and we were covered with a shower of dirt.

"They are setting up their barrage," the Lieutenant explained. "We'll have to go through it. Notice the next time a rocket goes up how our barbed-wire is cut so as to produce lanes through which we will go after we leap over the parapet." And then turning to his orderly, he ordered: "Go and find Ivan and bring him here!"

The orderly returned in a minute with a big burly fellow who saluted and stood at attention.

"This is Ivan," introduced the Lieutenant. "He is the under-officer commanding the stretcher-bearers of this company. You will go with him and when he returns, return with him!"

Then he turned to Ivan.

"Ivan," he said, "take the American doctor with you and take good care of him. Bring him back safe or I'll skin you alive!"

"*Tak tochena*—that surely, your Excellency," said Ivan, saluting.

I noticed that Ivan was entirely unarmed, carrying only a first aid kit slung over his shoulder. In fact, none of the stretcher-bearers were armed, and I realized what a self-sacrificing job theirs was—all take and no give. If a fellow is armed he feels much better when going into an attack, but the poor stretcher-bearer cannot think of his own safety at all. They can't even keep under cover by lying in shell-holes on the ground but must keep on carrying the wounded back just as though a couple of dozen machine-guns were not spraying the air full of death right behind them.

Ivan leaned against the trench parapet and lit a cigarette, and in the glow of the match which he held in his cupped hand to shield it from the wind I got a good glimpse of his face. He had a great red beard, fan-shaped like the tail of a grouse and matted with snow, a red nose and cheeks and little deep-set, gray eyes with bushy red eyebrows, peering out from under his white monkish head covering. It is queer how these little unimportant things impress you even when your mind is centered on bigger matters, and I can recall that kindly, homely peasant face now after two years as plainly as though it were yesterday, although I haven't seen it since.

I looked at my wrist-watch and saw by the illuminated dial it was 9:28—only seventeen minutes more.

I was trembling all over from suppressed excitement.

Looking through the loophole I could scarcely make out the German trenches through the whirling snow and flying smoke of exploding shells, even when the rockets flared, although they were only two hundred yards away across a slight depression in the ground. When a particularly great number of rockets lit up the snow-covered field I could just see a thicket of black stakes which marked their barbed wire. Here and there along this hedge great black splotches showed where our shells had hit, tearing up the snow and earth. Red flashes and clouds of smoke rose from where their trenches lay. A green rocket went up from their trenches and several machine-guns started to pound away, sounding like riveting machines on a sky-scraper at home, followed by the cracking of rifles all going like mad.

"They are getting nervous," said the Lieutenant at my elbow—in which respect, I thought, they were not much worse off than I.

I could hear ricochets spee overhead in the trees and the crack of bullets hitting the branches, and occasionally dirt would be thrown from the parapet of the trench as one struck not a foot above my head.

The small-arm fire gradually quieted down but did not entirely cease, a machine-gun sputtering nervously every now and then.

"How they must be straining their eyes trying to pierce the screen of whirling snow-flakes for the first movement in No Man's Land!" declared the Lieutenant. "The company on our left will go over a few seconds before we do. They have a little farther to go to where the German communicating-trench runs back. They must get back there to head the Boches off when they try to leave the salient that we will attack. You wait until the stretcher-bearers go forward—they will follow us—and stick close to Ivan!"

Two minutes more, my watch told me.

"Look to your left!" the Lieutenant shouted.

I looked but could see nothing but whirling snow in the flickering glare of the rockets.

"The company on the left went over," he said. "I heard their whistles."

He peered intently at his watch, holding a whistle to his lips.

Two shrill blasts and he crawled up over the parapet by means of one of the little ladders placed there for the purpose. He was followed by the white-draped figures of his men. They did not hurry but went carefully over, and as I looked down the line of the trench I could make out a few low-stooping figures passing slowly out through the lanes in the barbed wire. They were crawling and nearly invisible in their white garb. In a moment or two our sector was deserted except for the stretcher-bearers and reserves who were gazing out of their loopholes.

"Come!" said Ivan, and crawled up over the parapet.

I was in a daze. My brain felt numb. I was trembling all over but I followed with my heart thumping under my ribs.

As I stuck my head and shoulders over and looked out I saw three blood red rockets shoot up from the German lines on the left and then a dozen machine-guns started, together with a sharp volley of rifle fire, and the screech of shells. The wicked red flashes and the sharp stunning reports of their explosions indicated the starting of the German barrage through which we had to pass.

The red rockets were thrown up by the Germans, who had seen the attacking company on their right and were asking for an artillery barrage.

I followed Ivan's great stooping bulk as he scurried quickly through the barbed wire, half a dozen stretcher-bearers following at my heels.

There was a rip of tearing cloth and a stretcher-bearer swore softly as his white coat caught on the barbed wire. I could see nothing at all of the men of our company who had gone ahead. They were completely swallowed up in the swirling snow.

Ivan suddenly stopped and leaned over something white lying in the snow.

The stretcher-bearers crowded up about him, a sharp order was given, and the white object was placed groaning on the back of an orderly, who started running back toward our trenches with it. We sped on over the snow, the Germans now firing all along the line, and the din of the machine-guns and rifles was terrific. Every now and then shrapnel would explode overhead with a coughing *crump!* and I could hear the bullets hit the ground about me as I ran.

Ivan turned and ran left and then forward again, lifting his feet high over a mass of twisted wire and stakes. This was German wire torn by our artillery fire. He had found an opening and I followed him.

The firing directly in front of us was not so intense, but to the left, where the Germans were still throwing up their red rockets shrapnel, H E[4] shells and bombs were making a great row. I could hear voices—Russian words of command above the uproar.

Again Ivan stooped and another orderly went back with a limp form on his back.

---

[4] H E = high explosive—shells with strong steel casings, a bursting charge, and a fuse that detonates the bursting charge, shattering the case and sending out sharp cases (fragments or splinters) at high velocity.

Ivan started up over a ridge of earth covered with snow. He reached the top and stood poised a moment in the glare of a rocket. Then he coughed hollowly, swayed and slipped back, his great bulk crashing on top of me and carrying me down into a tangle of barbed wire.

As he fell, I thought of the bomb in my right hand. I felt something warm running down over my face as I squirmed out from under Ivan's body.

An orderly was bending over him.

"A bullet through the forehead, Excellency!" he reported. "He is quite dead, but I will take him back. Did they get you too?"

"Oh, no," I replied. "Take poor Ivan back." I wiped my sleeve over my wet face and the white cloth showed a dark stain, but, strangely enough, I felt no pain.

"*Sanitar! Sanitar!*"[5] a voice called from the darkness ahead.

I could see no one but crawled up cautiously over the ridge which I knew was the parapet of the German trench. I looked down over the parapet and saw two white-coated figures looking up at me.

"We have a wounded officer here," one of them said, as I slid over the parapet with the four remaining orderlies. He pointed to a third figure seated on the fire-step of the captured German trench. Two orderlies climbed back upon the parapet and we passed the wounded officer up to them.

"Be careful. It's his leg," one of the soldiers said.

When they had started back across No Man's Land with their burden, we went down the German trench toward the left.

I had gone only a few feet when I stumbled over a form lying in the darkness. As I stooped over it, one of the soldiers who was following me flashed an electric torch on the ashy face. It was a dead German with a small puncture in the throat from which a trickle of blood still oozed, and another in the chest.

"Bayonet!" commented an orderly at my elbow. We proceeded on up the trench and finally came to a number of steps which led down to a strongly built dug-out. I started to go down but was stopped by one of the soldiers.

"Don't go down without first throwing a bomb into the dug-out," he urged. "There may be Germans lurking there."

I threw the bomb which I had in my right hand through the open door, slipping the ring off the handle. A loud explosion shook the ground. A soldier flashed his searchlight over my shoulder as we entered the dug-out, which was filled with smoke from the bomb.

Through the gray veil of the little shaft of light, we searched about the dark interior and found in the center an overturned table and, in one corner, a crouching

---

[5] Orderly.

gray figure. The uniform was torn and soaked with blood. As I stepped toward it, the German weakly called: "*Kamerad!*"[6]

The German's face was covered with blood from a dozen small wounds which the bomb had made, but as he seemed able to walk we decided to take him with us.

The two orderlies led him out, escorting him by the arms; and when we had gained the trench, we found that we had over-stayed our time by two minutes. We clambered up over the German parapet and started back on the run over No Man's Land, the two orderlies dragging their prisoner with them.

The Germans were now throwing a strong barrage in No Man's Land. From their support trenches rockets flared and they began to shell the trenches we had just taken. One hit the parapet about forty yards away, showering us with dirt.

"I am hit in the arm!" exclaimed one of our men, but he changed his rifle to his other arm and went on.

We stooped low as we ran, and as I flew over the snow I had a queer feeling in my back—a feeling of expectancy as though something were going to hit me right between the shoulders—the sort of feeling you have when you're going down a dark, lonely road at night and you suddenly hear the patter of footsteps just behind you.

The orderlies and their prisoner were left far in the rear. In front of me I saw our barbed wire and I scurried along till I found an opening and plunged through, bumping into several other white-coats as I scrambled down over the parapet in a shower of loosened dirt. Then I sat down on the fire-steps gasping for breath. I think I had done the last 200 yards in less than nothing. Our men who had gotten safely back were talking excitedly.

"I ran him through and lifted him off his feet, my bayonet bent and he slid off," I heard one say. "Our bayonets ought to be stronger and thicker. See how it is bent."

I started up the trench and ran into Lieutenant Muhanoff.

"You are all right, I am so glad!" he exclaimed, grabbing me by the shoulders. "Ivan is dead—dum-dum bullet through the head. I feared something had happened to you. What is wrong with your face, you are covered with blood?" he asked as a rocket flickered.

He led me to a dug-out and held up a candle to my face.

"Strange, no wound. How did you get it?" he asked.

Then I remembered Ivan—how he had toppled over on me.

"Must be from Ivan," I said. "I was at his heels as he climbed over the parapet. He fell back on me and I felt something warm running down my face."

We were joined by several young officers who had taken part in the raid and their conversation reminded me of the dressing-room after a football game, when the team discusses the incidents of the game.

---

[6] Friend, mate, comrade.

"Our company on the left flank got off in the snow," said a boyish looking officer, his eyes glowing. "We could not see a thing. We went too far to the left and were late in shutting off the communication-trench. A lot of Germans escaped before we got there. You fellows in the other company got in before we did and drove them out. Say, how many machine-guns did we get?"

"Five."

"That's good; we'll have that many more in the regiment. And we got twenty prisoners, too." (The Russian regiments at that time averaged about 15 machine-guns to the regiment; the Germans had about 80 to the regiment.)[7]

"Yes, and we would have had more if your old company had not got lost. You fellows should not be allowed out after dark!"

We left them chatting away, and walked toward our dressing station. The Germans were still throwing rockets and pounding the section we had raided with H E shells.

"They are not certain whether we are still there or not," explained the Lieutenant.

"How many men did we lose?" I inquired.

"I think there were 8 killed and 45 wounded." At the dressing-station we found Nicholi Alexandrovitch bandaging the German we had taken from the dug-out.

"We have finished with eight of our wounded: they are now on their way back," said Nicholi. "The other regimental stations handled the other wounded."

The wounded German was a middle-aged man. He did not look very formidable. He was covered with small wounds from the exploding bomb. He looked so pathetic and helpless as he sat there having his numerous cuts touched with iodine that I felt sorry for him.

"I ran into the dug-out when the Russians entered our trenches," he said. "I could not get to an approach-trench as I heard the Russians ahead blocking my escape. I was hiding in the corner when there was a terrible explosion and I was driven up against the wall. Then some Russian soldiers came and brought me here."

I was glad he didn't recognize me, as I felt rather guilty about that bomb. His wounds, while numerous, were not dangerous and barring tetanus or blood-poisoning he would recover. He was soon bumping back over the rough roads in one of our ambulances bound for the division hospital. The Boche artillery was quieting down. Occasionally a machine-gun could be heard pounding out a few nervous shots, and then all would be quiet.

---

[7] This is a significant exaggeration of German machine gun capacity. Each division, which was comprised of four regiments, only had twenty-four machine guns. Russian machine guns were part of special machine gun detachments, four of which were assigned to a regiment, each of which had two guns. See Stephen Bull, *German Machine Guns of World War I* (New York: Osprey, 2016), and General Staff, War Office, *Handbook of the Russian Army, 1914*, 6th ed. (London: Imperial War Museum Department of Printed Books, 1996).

We sat down to discuss the night's work. Mike, his face beaming with smiles that I had returned safely, brought in the samovar, we lit our long fragrant cigarettes and leaned back in comfort. When Lieutenant Muhanoff rose to go I accompanied him to the door. The position lay as quiet as before the raid. There was an occasional rocket and a single rifle shot now and then, but that was all. The snow had stopped falling and the sky was clear. Great sparkling stars glared coldly in the black arch of the heavens and the wind murmured softly through the branches of the pines. It was hard to realize that a few hours ago this peaceful Russian forest had been a howling inferno.

Chapter X
I MEET THE CZAR

Weeks slipped by—weeks full of interest to me to whom everything was new. Every day there were a few wounded but not many, for both sides were sitting quietly waiting, waiting and filling up their regiments with reserves and their ammunition-dump with shells. New regiments were moved in every two weeks, but we stayed, working with each regiment of our division as it came out of reserve.

They would come stealing in at night—a long line of men in columns of fours, down the dark road through the forest. No talking was allowed and there wasn't a sound except their feet crunching the hard frozen snow, the occasional clank of a tin cup against an intrenching tool, subdued coughs, or a low word of command from an officer. There were long waits in the frosty air as they filed through the communication-trench by squads to the fire-trench to take up the positions of their tired comrades at the loopholes. The men who were released would come out through the communication-trenches in little groups, line up on the road beside the new regiment, and soon another regiment would have formed under the shelter of the pine-trees—bound for the billets a few miles to the rear. Off they would go silently till a mile or so back from the trenches. Then they would start one of their wonderful marching songs. I can hear them now as I write—the fine majestic swing, with the plaintiveness of the East in it, ringing out on the hard, cold air.

One day Colonel Kalpaschnecoff came in with the news that the Emperor Nicholas[1] was to visit our corps.

"There will be a big review of our troops who are in reserve," he said. "It will be worth seeing. The Emperor will stay at the staff for several days. You must come to the staff dinner and meet him."

The day before I was to ride back to the staff, Michael, my orderly, asked me if I cared to take a bath before I started. I had been bathing in a tin-basin not much larger than a soup plate.

---

[1] Tsar Nicholas II, who reigned 1894–1917, was the last emperor of Russia of the Romanov line. He relinquished the throne following the February Revolution in 1917, stepping down in favor of his younger brother Mikhail, who refused the crown. He was held under arrest until 1918, when he and his entire family were killed by the Bolsheviks during the Civil War.

Michael had always insisted upon helping me but he would shake his head and indicate his disapproval at such methods of ablution.

"That way no good, Meester," he would say in his pigeon English, as I balanced on one foot in the tiny basin, splashing the water about the dug-out. "Russian bath better."

"I know it's no good, Mike," I would reply, "but it's the best the country seems to afford."

"Meester, go with me to Russian bath, yes?" he persisted, when I asked him to get the hot water on this particular afternoon.

"Russian bath!" I exclaimed in astonishment. "How can I run up to Petrograd and be back to-morrow, Mike? What are you talking about?"

"Have Russian bath here—about one-half verst."[2]

"Why didn't you tell me that before?"

"I think Meester like American way better."

We started off, Mike leading the way, carrying soap, towels and clean clothes. Finally we came to two big dug-outs.

Steam was pouring from their crude chimneys and leaked out through the chinks of the doors, rising in clouds in the cold air. The door of one of the dug-outs suddenly opened and a gust of steam swirled out, from which emerged three figures clad in their birthday garments—big, husky Siberians with not a stitch on them. Steam rose from their wet, shining skin, which was almost the color of a fresh-boiled lobster. They rushed off into the deep snow, capering about in the drifts while I stood gazing at them in astonishment.

One dived into a snow-bank and kicked and rolled about while the others pelted each other with snow. I thought I had wandered into a madhouse. After romping about for several minutes, they dashed back with loud cries into the dug-out.

"Russian soldier takes bath," laconically remarked Mike.

"If you think I'm going to bathe in a snow drift, Mike, you're very much mistaken," I said. "Oh, no; only soldier does that. Siberian soldier very strong. No get sick."

We approached the other dug-out. Over the door a crude sign read "*Offetsersky Bonyah*"[3]—"Officers' Bath." We went down the steps and opened the door. It led into a room with a steaming atmosphere. The temperature was about 90° Fahrenheit. A large stove of rough masonry with a huge fire-box in which logs were burning, filled one end of the room. Several soldiers were piling on more wood.

Another door opened into a smaller room which was not so steamy nor hot. There were benches around the sides and pegs in the wall to hang clothes on. This

---

[2] An old Russian unit of measurement roughly equivalent to .66 miles (1.07 kilometers).

[3] *Ofitserskaia Bania*. A Russian bania is a traditional steam bath similar to a sauna.

was the dressing-room. Great drops of moisture dripped from the ceiling and walls on to the floor, which was made of close laid saplings hewn square.

We stripped and Mike opened the door which led into the bath-room proper. I stepped in. The room was frightfully hot. The other end of the great stove projected through the wall. Above the fire-box was an opening like an oven which was filled with stones. Beside the oven, placed so as to catch some of the heat, was a steaming kettle of water. At one end of the room I could see dimly through the vapor a series of step-like benches in tiers reaching almost to the ceiling. On the walls hung dippers and bundles of birch twigs tied together. A barrel of cold water completed the equipment.

Mike told me to sit on the bench. Then he dipped out a ladleful of water and threw it on the hot stones in the oven. With a loud hiss, a great volume of steam flooded the room, and I thought I would suffocate. He repeated the process and I thought I would parboil. Another attack and I felt that I was quite done and ready to serve! To my anguished mind he appeared as an imp of Satan, skipping about in the rolling clouds of vapor as he dodged back to avoid the first outpouring of the scalding stuff—at least his skin resembled that of an imp, a fine scarlet.

By this time I was sizzling. Every bit of moisture in my body seemed to be pouring out of my skin in droplets. I felt like a turkey being "basted."

Mike approached me with a basin of hot water and doused me with it. He made me lie full length on one of the planks while he soaped me and scrubbed me with a scrubbing brush. Then he poured more hot water on me, and seizing two of the bundles of birch switches proceeded to lay them on, one in each hand, beating a tattoo up and down my scalded back, stopping only to throw more water on the hot stones when the temperature of the room threatened to fall below 220°! Then he seized a bucket, plunged it in the barrel of icy water and let me have it. As I gasped and sputtered and writhed on the plank, he appropriately announced: "All finish!"

I reeled out of that chamber of horrors to the comparatively earthly temperature of the cooling room.

When I reached our dressing station, Nicholi rose as I entered the door and shaking my hand said politely: "I congratulate you!" I thanked him, stating that I too was glad to have survived the ordeal, but I afterward found out that such congratulations are customary in Russia and I can quite appreciate the origin of this ancient and sensible rite. Russian baths are like olives, however, and I soon became accustomed—or hardened—to them.

The next morning I rode my little Siberian pony back to the base near the staff. The Emperor's private train was to arrive at two o'clock at the station of Ceslivano, which was twenty miles away.

At twelve-thirty, General Pleschcoff went through the village in the Benz limousine-bound for the station to meet him. He was followed by an escort of a squadron of Cossack cavalry.

This motor, incidentally, formerly belonged to Prince Eitel Friederich[4] of Germany, son of the Kaiser. It was captured during the Germans' second attack on Warsaw by the soldiers of our First Siberian Army Corps. Our troop had broken through the German line in a counter-attack and some Cossacks attached to the corps got through to a considerable depth and nearly captured the Prince! His car had become stalled in the mud and he was forced to flee on horseback, abandoning the motor, which the Cossacks took and, with their ponies, hauled back to our lines.

It was a luxurious Benz limousine, upholstered in gray. When captured it contained a cut-glass vase filled with flowers, a lunch hamper with complete equipment of dishes, knives, forks and so forth, with the imperial crest engraved on them, and some bottles of wine, cigars and cigarettes, the latter bearing the Prince's initials and the Hohenzollern crest on them. On the door of the limousine was the imperial coat-of-arms in enamel. Some German officers were taken at the same time and they freely admitted that it was indeed the Prince's car. General Pleschcoff now used it as a staff car and I had many enjoyable rides in it.

Along the road leading to the station, at intervals of every hundred feet, soldiers were posted, and a platoon of cavalry was on guard at every cross-road. The snow covering the twenty miles of road had been scraped and shoveled into a fairly flat surface, and small pine trees had been cut and planted in the snow-drifts every twenty or thirty feet on both sides, forming an avenue which relieved the otherwise bleak and uninviting landscape.

These preparations had been going on for several days in anticipation of the visit of the Emperor.

We remained in the village, and at four-thirty o'clock a number of motor cars could be heard purring down the road. The sentries stood stiffly at attention as the car of the German prince but now bearing the Czar of all the Russias passed through the dusky street of the little village. We could not see him because it was nearly dark but we stood at attention in front of our cabin until he had passed.

A number of other staff motors passed, crowded with officers, and in front and in the rear of the motors the Cossack squadron rode at a brisk trot, the steam rising from their ponies in the frosty air.

That night the Emperor had dinner with General Pleschcoff privately and immediately afterword [sic] he retired to rest from his journey.

At the review the next day, an entire division, twenty-five thousand men, was drawn up in a large hollow square in the snow-covered field. At one end four regimental bands were massed. Our little organization, with its 180 orderlies, was lined up in one corner of the field.

It was very cold standing there in the open with the wind whirling clouds of powdery snow about. After about fifteen minutes, the staff motors drove up, the great

---

[4] Prince Eitel Friederich was the second son of Kaiser Wilhem II.

band struck up the Russian national anthem and twenty-five thousand voices took up its majestic strain.

The Emperor advanced into the middle of the square, followed by General Pleschcoff and a large body of officers. Every soldier stood at attention, and when the reviewing party had reached the center the band stopped and the Emperor spoke some words to the soldiers and then started down the long line of men, stopping at every company to shake hands with the officers.

As the Emperor passed down the line, the heads of the soldiers turned as though drawn toward him by a magnet, the Russian custom requiring every soldier to look the reviewing officer in the eye every moment. When the reviewing officer stands still and the troops pass by him the same rule is followed, so that when they get directly opposite him every head is turned sharply over the shoulder and snaps back like clockwork to a front gaze just as they pass him.

As the Emperor passed our corner I saw that he was dressed in the ordinary field uniform with the insignia of a colonel on his shoulder-straps. He wore the plain brown overcoat such as we all had on and a regular gray Persian-lambskin winter cap. He came up to Colonel Kalpaschnecoff, saluted, shook hands, and addressed a few friendly words to him in Russian, and passed on to where I stood with my hand to my cap in salute.

"Our new American doctor, Your Imperial Highness!" said General Pleschcoff.

"American doctor!" repeated the Emperor in perfect English, a kindly smile lighting up his face. "And you have come over here all the way from America to help our wounded?" he asked.

"Yes, Your Imperial Highness," I answered, in English.

"That is very fine, very good of you. We are very much in need of doctors," and he passed on.

He was a medium-sized man, erect and soldierly in bearing. His skin was a peculiar dusky red. He had large dark eyes—the kindest eyes I have ever seen.

He had a brown moustache and a neatly trimmed brown beard. There were a few streaks of gray in his beard and hair, and lines of care were beginning to show around his eyes and brow. He passed completely around the square. A group of priests clad in brilliant cloaks of gold and silver cloth, their long locks flowing in the wind, contrasted conspicuously with the dun-colored uniforms of a choir of soldiers. A long religious ceremony followed, during which everyone, including the Emperor, stood bareheaded in the cold—and it was perhaps five degrees below zero.

At times we all had to kneel in the snow while the priests chanted and the soldier choir sang the responses, their wonderful Russian voices sounding clear in the sparkling air.

It was a most impressive ceremony, the occasional far-off rumble of artillery adding to the effect.

In the great room at the staff that night, a throng of officers in uniforms glittering with decorations were gathered in groups, gaily chatting, when the door opened and the Emperor entered. A sudden hush fell on the noisy place and every man faced the door.

The Emperor went from group to group with General Pleschcoff, greeting each man cordially.

When he came to me, a friendly smile lit up his countenance.

"How do you like it here in the Russian army? Isn't the life too rough for you?" he asked. "We are a very simple people at best and our climate in winter is most trying, but I hope you are comfortable."

I told him that everything had been done to make me happy and that I was enjoying the life and the work very much. I noticed that the brick-red dusky coloration of his face, which I had thought in the afternoon might be due to the cold air of the reviewing field, still remained. He had a trick of nervously stroking back his moustache and then passing his hand to the side of his neck where the fingers would gently rub the skin. This was repeated on many occasions, particularly when he was absorbed in thought. He impressed me as an unassuming kind of man who would rather be in some secluded spot with his children than in the turmoil and ceremony of court life, and I think of him now, out there in the little Siberian town where he is in exile, not as a disappointed and unhappy man but rather as being content in the bosom of his family unburdened of the cares of state.[5]

At dinner, conversation flowed freely around the board without the least restraint, despite the fact that the ruler of the destinies of two hundred million people was seated there.

When we left the staff that night, Kalpaschnecoff remarked: "We all love the Emperor. Unfortunately he is surrounded in Petrograd by a crowd of men in which there is much pro-German influence. If he only had the strength of character that the Grand Duke Nicholas has, things would be better in Russia. When the Grand Duke was Commander-in-Chief, he was feared and at the same time loved by the army because he was always fair in his treatment of the soldiers even though he was a strict disciplinarian.[6] Our Emperor detests strife. He tries to smooth everything over. In-

---

[5] Following the Bolshevik seizure of power in the October Revolution in 1917, the tsar and his entire family were kept under house arrest in the city of Ekaterinburg, Siberia, until White forces attempting to defeat the Red Army began closing in on the city in July 1918. At that point, the Bolsheviks executed the tsar, his wife, and all of their children. The tsar's reputation as a dedicated family man who was much more comfortable as a private citizen than as emperor was widely known.

[6] This refers to the tsar's uncle, Grand Duke Nikolai Nikolaevich, who served as commander in chief from the start of the war until the disastrous "Great Retreat" in the summer of 1915, when the tsar himself replaced him in August.

stead of kicking out the German propagandists he is willing to endure them although he knows full well that they are the undoing of the nation."[7]

The Colonel's views were, of course, fully sustained by the events which followed.

---

[7] The view that German sympathizers were controlling affairs in Petrograd was widespread, though largely unfounded. See Fuller, *The Foe Within*.

Chapter XI
OVER THE GERMAN LINES

It was now past mid-winter. A foot and a half of snow covered the ground and the cold was intense, sometimes as low as fifteen degrees below zero.

The vast forest and swamps and fields through which the far-flung northern fighting line passed, lay sleeping white and desolate beneath the gray skies.

The two great armies apparently shared nature's lethargy, but they were not asleep. Always, day and night, they lay watching, waiting like two great beasts to spring at each other's throat. By day the aeroplanes winged their way through the frigid atmosphere, and by night the patrols crept out in No Man's Land seeking information concerning the enemy. Watching, waiting, not a battalion moved on the German side but what we knew it, and they were equally well informed of our maneuvers.

One cold night I was called to our aviation field to see one of our aviators who had been taken sick. I treated him for the next day or two and, by way of appreciation, he offered to take me across the lines in his machine someday if I wanted to go, although it was against orders. I told him I would certainly like to go if it wouldn't get him into any trouble; and some three weeks later I got a note from him telling me to be at his hangar at three P.M.

I found the Captain testing out a big two-seated machine in the snowy field.

"This was formerly a German plane," he explained. "We shot her down inside our lines and as she was not very much damaged, we fixed her up and are using her. She is of Albatross observation and bombing type—not very fast but big and steady."

He adjusted a fur-lined leather helmet to my head. It covered everything but my eyes.

"It will be very cold this evening, but the air conditions are good for flying. You sit here in the observer's seat," he said, pointing to a little cock-pit in the body of the machine back of the driver's seat. He adjusted the belt to my waist, strapping me in the seat. On a metal rail around the cock-pit was mounted a light machine-gun on a universal joint. Strapped alongside my seat under the decking was a carbine, such as our cavalry use.

"You may have to fire the carbine, if necessary," the Captain said, as he took his seat forward, "but of course you cannot operate the machine-gun. I have a couple of bombs underneath ready for dropping."

A mechanic spun the propeller and the motor started with a roar like a dozen machine-guns. Several soldiers held on to the wings to keep her from moving. The strong blasts of air shot back by the whirling propellers struck me in the face.

The Captain nodded his head, the soldiers let go and we started down the field.

Faster and faster we went. I looked over the edge of the cock-pit and ground was dropping out from under me. Down it went, objects shrinking in size as if by magic, the wire stays humming like a top as the air whistled through them. The motor roared and we dipped and we banked on a turn, spiralling upward.

Fields and forests and peasants' houses stood out like a relief map and the horizon momentarily receded as we soared higher and higher, enlarging our scope of vision.

After some minutes of upward circling, we headed straight for the west, where the golden sun was dipping beneath the edge of the earth. I suppose that we were at least 8,000 feet in the air. Things looked pretty small.

In a short time we were over the forest along the farther edge of which lay our trenches. On we flew, straight as an arrow, and presently I saw the "wall of Troy" effect where our trenches emerged in spots from the edge of the forest. Across a little open space of field, which I knew to be No Man's Land, I could see the German lines with their zigzag approach trenches.

As we passed them, I saw a yellow-brown puff of smoke in the air far below and off to the right. Several others appeared as though by magic, and then above the roar of the motor I heard a faint *put-put*—the explosion of German anti-aircraft shrapnel—they were shooting at us.

Roads ran straggling off through the forest and over the fields like black threads on a white cloth. A group of gray dots directly on one of these roads scattered and disappeared under the sheltering trees bordering on the road. I knew that they were German soldiers getting under cover fearing that we would spot them and drop a bomb on them. They reminded me of chickens at home when a hawk would float over them.

More brown puffs of smoke appeared, some fairly close and others far away, as the Germans increased their fire on us.

I was not alarmed—those little brown puffs looked so harmless—and the fact that I could hear their explosion only faintly made them appear less dangerous than they otherwise would have done.

Soon, however, the Germans began to get the range better and then the Captain dipped and I was looking down over his head straight toward the earth for a second or so. I felt as if we were falling: my stomach seemed rising into my chest. Then we assumed the horizontal again.

By dropping several thousand feet we got under the German shrapnel which now burst harmlessly above us as we turned and flew directly north paralleling the German lines.

Below I saw a group of gray squares, the thatched roofs of peasant huts, from which the snow had melted. When we were directly over the village, the Captain pointed down with his hand over the side, indicating that I should watch closely, and then reached down and manipulated something near his feet.

I looked over the side and saw a dark object flash down under the machine for an instant and then disappear as the machine lurched slightly. A great white mushroom-shaped cloud rolled up from the center of the village. The Captain had dropped one of his bombs, suspecting, as I learned later, that the staff of a German division was located in one of the larger houses of this village. As we moved on I looked back and saw smoke pouring up from the village, indicating that a house was on fire.

The sun was now below the horizon and the earth under us was growing dusky and objects indistinct. We headed east toward our lines, the golden afterglow at our backs.

We were some miles back of the German lines at a height of about 10,000 feet, I should judge, when the motor suddenly stopped. The wind whistled just the same through the cordage but the monotonous roar of the motor was gone.

The Captain leaned forward, hastily working on something on the dashboard in front of us. The nose of the machine was turned slightly toward the ground. I did not realize our danger until the Captain shouted: "We are in for it now—motor dead—don't know whether I can plane back to our lines—or not!"

In the gathering gloom below, I saw several red flashes stab upward: then I heard a screech and several distinct explosions above us and to the right. With the motor dead, it was easy to hear the coughing report of the German shrapnel. The earth seemed gradually to float up as we glided swiftly down and forward toward the lines.

Could we make it?

There was no wind to help us. The Captain devoted all his attention to the machine. Again and again he tried to start the motor, but she remained silent. He was getting all the forward movement he could with a minimum waste in altitude, peering intently through the gloom for a glimpse of the trenches.

I pictured myself a prisoner in Germany or hanging by a rib to the top of a pine-tree, for fields suitable for landing were few and far between. Ahead the forest was broken by a gap. Perhaps, I thought, it was No Man's Land.

We were whirling down perilously close to the tops of the pines and I knew that machine-guns and rifle bullets could easily reach us as we crossed the lines. Fortunately the motor was quiet as we rushed along, so that we flew silently and would not be so apt to attract attention.

There was a loud explosion below and the machine lurched drunkenly—the Captain had dropped the remaining bomb in the first part of the German lines because it was too dangerous to carry, as we did not know what sort of landing we would make.

We were now crossing the open space. I could see the German trenches below quite distinctly, and a slight crackling sound like fire in dry grass came up to me as they sniped at us with rifles and machine-guns.

Beyond the open space of No Man's Land stretched the black wall of our forest barring the way. We headed for it and then veered sharply to the left, and I saw the Captain's objective—there was a tiny clearing beyond a gap in the forest where the trees were not so tall.

We got over our lines and headed for this clearing. If we could just scrape over the scrub pines, we could make a landing. With great skill and judgment, the Captain elevated her nose, perilously lessening her momentum, for if we slowed down too much we would have a lateral or tail dive and be dashed to pieces. He dipped again and I could almost touch the tops of the pines as we shot over them. Then he raised her nose, we skimmed a spiked top, and were clear of the trees. We glided down into the center of that little clearing, bouncing along over the uneven ground and finally stopped. We both sat still a moment.

The Captain crossed himself and I knew he was murmuring a little prayer of thanks.

A soldier came running out of the forest, his rifle held ready to fire, because in the dark he could not tell whether we were friend or foe.

"All right, Galoopchick!" sang out the Captain. "Don't shoot: we are Russians!"

When the soldier came up we found that we had landed in the territory back of the lines held by the 5th regiment of our corps—about two miles north of our dressing station and half a mile back of the first line trenches.

The report the Captain made out at our dressing station, at which he stopped for a moment or two, revealed to me what training and practice in aerial observation can accomplish. I have set down nearly everything I saw while above the German lines, and my eyes are far better than the average, but the Captain reported the location of two new German batteries; the reoccupation of a dug-out village by a new regiment of German troops in reserve; the fact that the Germans were using a certain field for the drilling of troops in reserve; and that field kitchens were brought up at dusk on a road which could be easily reached by our artillery.

No wonder the air has played such an important part in this war!

Chapter XII
THROUGH A SHOWER OF SHELLS

Signs of unusual activity in the corps began to develop as the middle of February was reached. The days were growing longer, and while the cold was just as intense one felt that the backbone of the winter was broken.

The aeroplanes droned across the sky more frequently, and the transport was bringing up great supplies of ammunitions and stowing them in the shell-dumps.

One day a German aeroplane flew over our lines and dropped circulars printed in Russian which stated that the Germans knew we were to make an offensive, that they were aware of all the preparations we were making and were driving up reserves in men and artillery to check any attack we might make. The pamphlet even went so far as to say: "We are aware that you will attack on March 6th, 1916, Russian style."[1]

These circulars were dropped about February 10th—Russian style—which is thirteen days later than our new style.[2]

We were amused at these announcements, considering them just German bluff, and yet we could feel something was really in the air.

Orders came that the entire army corps was to move to a new position about ten miles farther south.[3] We started for our new base on February 27th and found the roads choked with new troops coming in to replace our corps. For miles they stretched across the frozen landscape. The roads were like huge brown arteries through which flowed slowly moving columns of men, artillery and transports, ebbing on endlessly to replace our corps—a constant stream of gray-brown.

By March 2nd we were in the trenches taking the place of a Caucasian division which had been holding them all the winter.

All this time a great concentration of artillery was taking place directly in the rear of our new lines. Huge 9-inch and 6-inch guns came lumbering through the village. The roads had not yet begun to thaw and they were easy to move. Endless columns of caissons loaded with shells rattled back and forth bringing up shells to fill

---

[1] Russian style refers to the calendar used in Russia prior to 1918, which was the Julian calendar adopted by Tsar Peter the Great in the early eighteenth century.

[2] This is incorrect. The Russian calendar was thirteen days *behind* the Western one.

[3] The entire corps was transferred to the staff of the Second Army, under which it remained until July 1916.

their gaping throats. The Russian officers were overjoyed at the immense amount of big guns and ammunition available. They were at last to meet the Germans on an almost equal footing.

"At last we have enough artillery!" exclaimed Lieutenant Muhanoff excitedly one day, rushing into the cabin where we had our base. "We'll give them a pounding and walk right through to Vilna."

Everybody felt equally optimistic, for we heard that General Pleschcoff had been given five army corps to command. They were placed on a front of about 35 kilometers, three in the line and two in reserve.

This was apparently true, for already near our base a reserve army corps of 40,000 men was in billet in numerous little villages and dug-out towns. A division of Cossack cavalry had also been brought up and held in reserve in case we broke through.

There was no question that a big battle was impending. The heavy guns which had reached their positions were heard every day getting the range of the German positions.

On March 3rd I visited the trenches to pick out advanced and main dressing stations in our first division.

The trenches were again at the edge of a great forest, facing across a flat open field, across which was another great forest of pines. The German trenches were on the edge of the latter. The field was about a quarter of a mile wide without a bit of cover.

The new ground differed from that which we had occupied to the north in that it was simply a great swamp. The trenches were dug in only about two feet. There was a thick covering of ice on the bottom. To make up for their lack of depth, they had been built up in front with banks of dirt and sod. On account of the swampy character of the ground, very few dug-outs had been constructed and not one fit for use was at our disposal. We had to work in tents covered with pine boughs to hide them from observation.

It gave promise of being very nasty, dangerous work. The only protection we had from the German artillery were the tree-trunks.

Our batteries were grouped in the forest.

There seemed to be hundreds of them, the three inch guns being close to the line, the heavier pieces two or three kilometers back. One light battery was up within a hundred and fifty yards of the first line trenches.

As I walked through the forest, I would come upon battery after battery cleverly concealed in the underbrush. A few hundred feet back of the spot I picked for the main dressing station, located about a third of a mile behind the trenches, were grouped sixteen three-inch guns in a line not twenty feet apart.

I did not like having the dressing station so near, but there was no other place available. In this war, strictly military matters have first choice—the care of the wounded is a secondary consideration.

I dropped in to see the commander of one of the batteries who was known throughout the corps as one of the best artillery officers in the army, although he was a queer old character. He had been wounded on three occasions earlier in the war and had the reputation of being a regular old fire eater. He was pop-eyed and had a little beard under his chin, and resembled very much a patriarchal old billy-goat.

He always kept two milk cows with his battery because he wouldn't drink his tea without milk. I had just passed them, stolidly munching hay, tied to trees near the battery. He also carried an old brassy graphophone with him wherever he went.

His men had built him a small hut of logs and dirt, heated by a charcoal brazier. I pushed aside the piece of canvas which served as a door and looked in.

He was sitting hunched up over the brazier, his fur coat buttoned tight up around his neck and his bulging eyes glowing in the light of a candle stuck in the neck of an empty bottle as he pored over a map. The interior of the hut was not much larger than a dog kennel but the graphophone was there standing on a block of wood.

"Come in! Come in! Close the door: it is cold!" he bawled. He always shouted at me, evidently thinking that the difficulty I had in understanding Russian was an indication that I was hard-of-hearing, although, as a matter of fact, he had undoubtedly acquired the habit of talking loudly from the necessities of his work when his batteries were in action.

"Well, Colonel," I said, "I see you are all fixed up to give the Germans a serenade!"

"Serenade! We're going to blow them to hell: we're going to blow them to hell!" he shouted. "They've concentrated a number of batteries in a clump of trees no larger than my hand. We're going to let them have a hundred guns steadily until we have mowed down trees, batteries and everything! You won't find anything left but scrap-iron when we finish."

"Do you think the Germans know we're going to attack?" I asked.

"Know it!" he yelled. "They know the exact minute it is to come off—which is more than I do. I don't even know what day it is to be. They knew long ago—as soon as it was planned in Petrograd."

He was so excited that the veins on his forehead stood out like cords and his face was purple. I returned to our base, and the next day we brought down the ambulances and several wagons carrying three tents, one large and two small, surgical material, three small stoves, provision and horse feed.

We made quite a long column. As we approached our destination we had to go over a road which ran across an open field and which was exposed to the German observers. It was about 3 P. M. and quite light.

"I should advise your Excellency[4] not to cross till dark," advised a sentry. "The Germans have shelled everyone who has crossed today."

It was a good mile to the screening forest beyond. Not a living thing could be seen on the road, but here and there I could make out the dead bodies of horses lying sprawled out on the road with their legs sticking stiffly in the air.

"All the transport and artillery were brought up at night," the sentry continued, "and today only single wagons or a small group of men at a time have been allowed to cross."

I had been ordered to have my dressing station in order by the next morning, however, and as I could not very well fix things up in the dark, I decided to take a chance despite the sentry's warning.

I told the drivers to allow a good space between each wagon and to cross at a brisk trot, whipping up their horses and galloping as rapidly as possible to the other side if we were shelled.

We were half-way across and I was congratulating myself on our good fortune when I heard a warning screech in the air as a shell passed over our heads. It burst with a loud report, throwing up a fountain of black smoke and dirt in a field about four hundred yards beyond, and the drivers whipped up their horses and galloped for dear life, the little two-wheeled ambulances bouncing over the frozen road.

The travelling kitchen was not so fortunate. It was very heavy and the horses could move only at a trot. The drivers yelled as only Russian drivers can and waved their long whips in the air but the horses needed no urging when a second shell came in with a *whiz-bang!*—this time only two hundred yards beyond the road. Then a yellow puff of smoke appeared in the air ahead and a shrapnel shell coughed out its pellets, making the snow fly up in little spurts in the field just beyond the road.

We were flying along at this time and several more high explosives came over, but all burst beyond the road. We galloped behind a little rise of ground which hid us from the view of the German observer and we had no more shells for a couple of minutes. When we emerged from the little knoll, however, the Germans were waiting for us and a shell screeched down and burst not a hundred feet ahead of my horse. I crouched low on the horse's neck, expecting to be hit, but nothing happened. Another hundred yards and we were safely in the forest. The wagons came bouncing in under the trees and the drivers laughed excitedly, but I noticed that the faces of many of them were pale. I am sure mine was.

That evening we hastily set up our dressing station. The small tents for the advance dressing station were placed in the forest about a hundred yards back of the first line trenches. We covered them completely with the branches of pine-trees to hide

---

[4] Prior to the February Revolution of 1917 that brought down the tsarist regime, soldiers in the Russian Imperial Army addressed officers with this highly respectful honorific, as well as using the formal "you," while officers used the informal form with soldiers. This was a cause of significant resentment among some rank-and-file.

them from the Germans. We placed the large tent a third of a mile back along the road, near the old Colonel's battery. This was to be the main dressing station where the ambulances would meet the stretcher-bearers when they carried the wounded back from the advance dressing station. Horses and ambulances were parked under the trees near the main dressing station. We had a little charcoal stove in each tent. Wood could not be used, as the smoke would have attracted German fire.

The night of the fifth of March was intensely cold. A foot of snow covered the ground. The troops who were billeted in the forest in reserve, however, had no tents and had to sleep in the snow, for there were few dug-outs on account of the marshy nature of the ground. Most of them had to be content with shelters built of brush to shield them from the biting wind where, without blankets, they sat about, crouched over little charcoal fires in the snow.

The Russian soldier is not provided with a blanket—his overcoat of medium-weight having to serve instead. He has underwear of cotton muslin. This, with a pair of heavy trousers and a fairly heavy shirt, or *ruboshka*,[5] is all he has to protect him from the biting cold of an almost arctic climate.

Despite their sufferings, the soldiers in reserve were extremely patient. Not a complaint was heard.[6] Were they not going to break through the German lines and drive the invader out of Holy Russia?

They sat about in little groups singing softly, for the Germans must not hear them, huddled close together for warmth. Some were drying out their foot-gear, holding over the glowing embers of their fires the long strips of cloth which they use in place of socks.

I felt sorry for them at first because they had no socks and asked one old bearded stretcher bearer who was engaged in the drying-out process if his feet did not become cold without socks.

"We don't like socks," he replied. "We wrap this long cloth around the foot and leg and then slide into our boots. When the foot becomes wet we turn the cloth end for end, wrapping the wet part around the leg, where it dries quickly, while the dry end is wrapped around the foot and keeps it warm."

I have since learned that the German soldiers have in many instances abandoned the sock for this more primitive but sensible article.

That night I slept in the main dressing station on a pallet of fresh pine boughs, wrapped up in my sleeping bag. As I went to sleep I heard the Colonel's old graph-

---

[5] *Rubashka*.

[6] Another standard trope of the time concerning Russian soldiers: patient, long-suffering, rarely complaining.

ophone grinding out the strains of the Berceuse from *Joselyn*,[7] punctuated at certain points by an ear-splitting crash from one of his three-inchers and the drone of a shell overhead as he sent the Nemets a good-night message.

---

[7] *Joselyn* is an opera by composer Benjamin Godard, based on a poem by Alphonse de Lamertine. The Berceuse is a part of the piece that resembles a lullaby, and was very popular at the time, sung by famous tenors.

Chapter XIII
THE BATTLE OF POSTOVY[1]

On March 6th, at nine o'clock in the morning, our artillery opened up a terrific fire on the German barbed wire, fire-line trenches, and such batteries as had been spotted by our aeroplanes. I went down into our first-line trenches, which were half filled with icy snow and muddy water coming up almost to my knees, and peered out through a loophole toward the German trenches. The black line of forest along which his first line ran was almost hidden by spurting clouds of smoke and dirt. A gray haze simply hid them from view where the high explosive shells tore up barbed wire and trench parapets.

The crashing of our guns was incessant, producing the sound known as "drum-fire," and the shells screeched and hummed overhead in a steady procession. The German batteries were replying, firing principally on our batteries and the reserve positions, where the troops were lying in the forest unprotected by trenches.

Occasionally machine-guns and rifles would burst forth in a crackling volley as they became nervous, but most of the time the rifle fire amounted only to the isolated shots of snipers.

I went to one of our advance dressing stations where a few wounded men struck by shrapnel were coming in from the reserve positions and were being bandaged and sent to the main dressing station, the heavily wounded being carried by our orderlies on stretchers, where they met the ambulances and were conveyed to the division hospital six miles in the rear.

The work was being carried on here satisfactorily, and I started for the other dressing station a few hundred yards away in the forest. I was passing a huge pine-tree when I heard a voice from far overhead, faint above the roar of artillery, crying: "Meester! Meester!"

---

[1] This was part of a larger operation known as the Lake Naroch Offensive, launched at the request of Russia's ally, France, which hoped it would draw some German units away from the fighting in western Europe. It was conducted by the Russian Second Army against the German Tenth Army and lasted from March 17–30 (5–17, Old Style) and was largely unsuccessful for the Russians, who sustained losses of over 76,000. For a full account of the offensive, see N. E. Podorozhnyi, *Narochskaia operatsiia v marte 1916 g.* (Moscow: Gos. voennoizdatel´svo Narkomata oborony, 1938). Available online at http://grwar.ru/library/Podorozhnyi-Naroch/index.html.

I looked up, and high up in the topmost branches, screened by the thick boughs, I made out an artillery officer perched on a little scaffolding nailed to the tree. He held a field telephone in his hand. The wires ran down the tree and off to the rear towards his battery. He was an observer, spotting the hits of the shells from his battery and correcting the range of the guns from his lofty perch. It was the same young officer whom I had seen in the observation point in the trenches on my first visit to them—the one who was so anxious to get the Boches who were fleeing from the old building in No Man's Land.

He leaned far out from his dizzy perch, his face showing white against the dark foliage of the trees, and cupping his hands to his mouth, shouted down to me: "Will you send an orderly up to me with a pail of hot tea? I am very cold up—"

A strange, awful change came over his countenance. As though by magic, a tiny dark spot appeared on his forehead just above his right eye—like the dark spot which appears on the white surface of a target in a shooting-gallery after the crack of a rifle. His lower jaw dropped, he grinned hideously down at me and then, very slowly, he began to sway forward. His arms dropped, the field telephone fell from his hands and hung dangling by its wire, and his body pitched forward off his seat and came crashing down through the branches, bouncing as it hit the thick limbs, inert and limp as a bag of meal, and fell with a sickening thud at my feet.

I lifted the head, turning it so that I could see the face. It was crimson with blood pouring from the small dark hole just above the eyebrow. A bullet, possibly a wild bullet or one from the rifle of a sniper who had seen him through binoculars, had killed him instantly. That evening they buried him in the forest near the dressing station.

The artillery kept up its fire and we expected it to continue until the next day. We decided that the Germans had been one day wrong in their prediction and we felt sure the artillery would spend at least eighteen hours in destroying the German barbed wire and machine-gun emplacements.

About mid-day, however, we were astonished to receive word that the troops would go over the top at three that afternoon. The Germans were correct after all! More amazing to us than the accuracy of the German prediction was the fact that the Russian general staff had not changed the date of the attack after these notices had been dropped by the Germans.

That only six hours' artillery preparation was ordered was also surprising to us, and many of the younger officers predicted that our troops would run their heads into a stone wall.[2]

The German shrapnel was bursting over the trees and the H E shells were tearing things up as I made my way cautiously into the first line trenches about 2:30 P. M.

---

[2] In actuality, the Russian's initial artillery bombardment lasted two full days, but it did not have the intended effect, leaving much of the German artillery undamaged.

The trenches were full of soldiers crouched down below the low parapets up to their knees in icy water and mud, waiting for the signal to go over the top.

I found Lieutenant Muhanoff with his company. He was smoking a cigarette and did not appear at all nervous at the impending action.

"We will just walk over and take the first couple of lines," he declared confidently. "Look at that artillery tearing them up. There won't be a man left in that trench," and through a loophole we could see that their first line was a welter of flying smoke and dirt.

"I have here in this packet some money and a ring which belonged to my father," he said, handing me a sealed and addressed paper package. "Will you see that it gets to my mother in Smolensk in case I don't come back?"

"Nonsense!" I exclaimed. "Of course you will come back! But I'll take the package and see that your mother receives it if you don't."

"Thank you, dear friend," he replied. "And now, good-bye! It is two minutes of three and I must get my men up, ready to go over."

He walked away and spoke quietly to his men, where they sat about in little groups on the fire step of the trench. He was beloved by all his soldiers and as they lined up along the trench wall I felt that they would follow him to hell if necessary.

A shrill whistle sounded up and down the trench and they swarmed up the little ladders and ran, stooping low, through the passages cut in the barbed wire. Lieutenant Muhanoff gaily waved his hand to me as he leaped on the parapet. Long brown lines of men advancing in successive waves went quickly across the snow-covered field with loud "Hurrahs!" their bayonets flashing in the setting sun.

They were hardly over the top when the German machine-guns and rifles turned a withering fire on them, the machine-guns hammering and the rifles crackling.

Across the flat, white field they went, and every here and there a man would go down sprawling in the snow. The German barrage fire appeared as a haze of whirling smoke and dirt, partly hiding them as they went through it, and the earth shook with the violence of the explosions. The sprawling forms were like the foam that a receding wave leaves on the sand as it sweeps back to its parent sea. Many came running or crawling back with all manner of wounds, as the advancing line became lost to sight in the tumbling, rolling fog of the barrage; but No Man's Land was covered with men who would never move again. I hurried back to the dressing station, for I knew there would be much work to do. Rumors reached us there as we worked—wild stories told by the wounded.

Some said we had broken through the German defense, others that we had captured four lines of their trenches, while still others insisted that we had not even taken the first line trench, our attack having broken down and our men having been forced to retreat.

The latter report proved to be the correct one, much to our sorrow.

The firing quieted down slightly and Lieutenant Muhanoff came to the tent where I was wading about in a sea of wrecked humanity—a groaning, writhing sea lying there on the snow—working hurriedly to patch them up for the stretcher-bearers to carry back to the main dressing station where the ambulances were.

The Lieutenant looked as if he had been in a prize fight. His face was swollen and discolored, his glasses were gone, one eye was nearly closed, a cut gaped on his forehead, and his clothing was torn and bloody.

"What's the matter? Have you been boxing?" I asked.

"Yes; that's just about what you would call it. When we got over to their first line, there was hardly a German in it—only machine-gun crews and a few rifle men, and what was left of my company quickly disposed of them with the bayonet. I started for the second line when I saw that we had easily won the first line, thinking that my men were following me. When I mounted the parapet of their support-trench, I saw it was full of Germans, but I jumped in, firing my revolver as I leaped, and then I realized for the first time that I was alone!

"There were about fifteen Germans in that particular sector of the trench and they jumped on me without any ceremony. One big fellow knocked me down with a blow from his rifle and the rest piled on me, pinning me to the ground and pummeling me with their fists, for the confusion was so great and the trench was so close-packed that they could not use their bayonets.

"I thought I was gone, when over the parapet leaped ten of my Siberians. They went at those Germans with their bayonets as well as they could, but the fighting was so close that it was more like an ordinary bar-room brawl, and after a great deal of hammer and tongs fighting, six of us finally broke loose and started back to the first line trench; but only four got back here, the other two being killed by machine-gun fire en route."

"How about the four others that jumped into the trench?" I asked.

"They were killed right there!"

"And how many Germans did you fellows account for?"

"I don't know exactly. They lay around pretty thick, but some of them ran up the trench when my soldiers came over: they don't like our long bayonets."

"How did your men know you were in danger?"

"One of them had seen me disappear over the parapet and thought I had been taken prisoner. He got nine of his comrades together and they charged the trench to rescue me. It was a pretty brave thing to do, for they did not know how many Germans were there. The attack has been a failure, however. Of my company of two hundred men, only forty got back uninjured when we got the order to give up the captured line and retire. We were undoubtedly betrayed in this attack. The enemy had hundreds and hundreds of machine-guns in that first line all ready and waiting for us!"

He was greatly discouraged and downcast as I bound up the cut on his forehead.

All that evening our artillery kept pounding away and reserve troops were brought up to replace the shattered regiments who had been in the attack in the afternoon. They had suffered frightful losses. One regiment which had had four thousand men only a few hours before now had only about eight hundred![3]

I went back to the main dressing station, which was swamped with wounded. Our forty ambulances, which could carry only two wounded lying down or four sitting up, were inadequate for the task of carrying them all back to the division hospital. The roads were frightful and the drivers had to walk their horses the entire distance, for even when they went slowly and carefully the suffering of the wounded as they bounced about in those rough carts was terrible.

Their route along the road was accompanied by heart-rending cries of agony which could be heard several hundred yards from the roadside. The cold was intense, and as our tent could not accommodate all the wounded, many had to lie in the snow wrapped in such poor blankets as we could supply. At times there were as many as a hundred lying in the snow outside the tent, many of them having only their wet overcoats to protect them against the cold!

During the evening, I had a great many emergency operations to do. I was operating on one poor fellow who had had a leg completely torn off by a shell fragment. Bright red streams of blood were spurting from several arteries in the torn stump and it was necessary to catch the bleeding vessels with delicate forceps and tie them up with strands of catgut. Great haste and a steady hand were necessary to complete the work in time to save his life. He was lying on the raised stretcher which served as an operating table and Nicholi was giving ether. Metia was in one of the advance dressing stations. I had no other trained assistants.

A new orderly, who had been in the army only a few days before this big fight and who had never been under shell fire, was holding a candle so that I could see to catch the elusive arteries with the forceps. We could use no other light for fear it would attract the attention of the enemy and bring a shower of shells from their artillery on the many wounded who lay about the tent.

Arteries are elastic and when cut recede into the tissues as if they were made of rubber. It was difficult to find them in the flickering light of the candle, and the life blood of the soldier, whose pulse I could scarcely feel, was fast ebbing away. Those bleeding points had to be stopped at once or he would die.

I was trying desperately to catch one of the arteries which was throwing a bright red jet of blood into my face as I leaned over when I heard the screeching approach of a German shell. It seemed to be coming straight down on the tent—one of those big howitzer shells with a high trajectory coming from far up in the sky. I could hear it for a long time—at least it seemed a long time although in reality only a matter of seconds.

---

[3] Russian losses were more than 7,000 on the first day of the attack.

The new orderly heard it too and his hand began to shake. The nearer the shell came the worse it shook, and when the shell exploded close to the tent and great jagged pieces came humming and tearing their way through the canvas above our heads, he gave a convulsive shudder and dropped the candle and we were in darkness. I called sharply for a light and he fumbled around and found a match and got the candle going again. All the time the wounded man was bleeding furiously.

The orderly was a great hulking fellow, well over six feet in height, and he must have weighed two hundred and forty pounds.

I had found several of those large bleeders and tied them when I heard another of those infernal shells coming again. Once more the candle started to shake and once more we were in darkness when the shell burst. My nerves were now gone with the effort of controlling my own hands and keeping them from trembling, for the work was so fine that a tremor would have defeated my purpose. I was badly frightened myself and it was only by a great effort that I kept my hands steady. The second shell had hit so close that the tent rocked with the concussion and cold air was pouring in through numerous jagged rents. I dismissed the orderly and shouted for Michael to come in. He was outside, helping to load wounded into the ambulances. Mike proved to be more hardened and when the next shell came in we at least had light to work by. We finally checked the bleeding and started the wounded man back for the divisional hospital, well wrapped in blankets, with enough of the precious life-blood in his body to keep him going till he reached the point where further restorative measures could be applied.

Chapter XIV
THE DOGS OF WAR

The big German guns were shelling the Colonel's double battery, which, as I have mentioned, was located very near our tent. They were unable to silence either the battery or the Colonel, for I could hear his voice bawling out orders to his men above the roar of hundreds of guns and the screech of flying shells. Sometimes he would let go with his entire sixteen guns simultaneously. At other times he would fire them one after the other in rapid succession.

The muzzles of the guns were pointed directly at our tent, the shells flying not a hundred feet above our ridge-pole, and when he fired a salvo the tent-wall would actually bulge in on the side toward the battery, candles would be extinguished, and my head, which was splitting from the noise, would rock from the concussion.

The wounded who were now brought in by our bearers were in frightful condition. They were the heavily wounded who had been lying in the snow in No Man's Land unable to move. There were many abdominal and brain wounds and all of them were nearly frozen from the cold.

As night came on, our bearers would crawl cautiously out between the lines and search in the darkness for these poor fellows. Occasionally a German machine-gun would break forth in a spasm of firing. This meant that they had detected a searching party and had turned a machine-gun on them, or, in the flare of a rocket, they had seen some wounded Russian dragging himself painfully over the snow. They take no chances in allowing wounded to get back to their own lines.

We had with us three Airedale terriers. They were trained to locate the wounded in thickets and brushy places where they could not be seen by our searching parties, who, for obvious reasons, cannot carry any light.

About two o'clock we received word that a wounded man had managed to crawl in from between the lines and had reported that some badly wounded soldiers were lying in a thicket and were perishing in the cold. He had passed several of them as he crawled painfully by. They were too weak to move but displayed signs of life.

I summoned the three orderlies who had charge of the dogs, and, taking twelve stretcher-bearers, hurried to our trenches opposite the point indicated. The weather had moderated slightly and the snow was melting a little, but it was one of those damp, penetrating nights when the cold seems to go right through to the bone.

As we splashed through a communication trench, the dogs tugging at their leashes, I thought of those poor devils lying out there, suffering all kinds of anguish and without any hope of being rescued.

It was as dark as a pit as we entered the first line trenches. They were full of soldiers sitting about shivering in the cold and waiting for the next order to attack.

In the occasional flicker of a rocket I could make out, half-way between our trenches and the Germans', a dark patch of scrubby weeds and stunted bushes. In this little thicket lay the wounded.

The orderlies who had charge of the dogs lifted them up on the parapet, unsnapped their leashes, and spoke a sharp word of command: "Begone!"

The dogs disappeared in the darkness of No Man's Land and were gone for quite a long time. I thought at first that they must have gone astray or that one of those scattering volleys from the German trenches had ended their mission of rescue.

Tang!

Something in our entanglements had struck a projecting piece of wire directly in front of me. A rocket shot up, and over the parapet a yard to my right I saw a shaggy head peering down. The dog held something in his mouth. I heard him whine softly. One of the orderlies reached up to get him and he snarled savagely and jumped back.

It was not his master and he was trained when on duty to keep away from any other person. Another orderly stepped up on the fire-step and spoke to him, and he whimpered softly and came to his master, who lifted him down.

In the light of my electric torch I saw that he held in his mouth a crumpled, blood-stained cap. His master took the cap in his hand, snapped the leash on the dog's collar, lifted him up on the parapet and crawled up after him, followed by two stretcher-bearers.

The dog led them out through the barbed wire, tugging at his leash, and I followed the little party, curious to see whether he would find the owner of that cap.

I could distinguish their dim forms as they crawled on hands and knees, dragging the rolled up stretcher after them. I followed, also crawling, and when a rocket soared up and cast its ghostly light over the field, we all "froze," lying perfectly flat in the snow until the light died out. I heard the dry grass crackle as they wormed their way into the thicket and I thought that we must be very close to the German lines. Several bullets struck the weeds about me.

My hand touched something which felt like a piece of woolen cloth in the weeds and I saw a dark object lying partly concealed in the thicket. I reached out and felt a human arm—it was hard and stiff and the clutched hand was icy. I tried to move the arm, but it was rigid and I knew that there was no life in that cold body.

I crawled hurriedly on through the bush and found the little party kneeling about another dark object sprawled in the snow. The body was still warm but the hands were very cold and at the wrist I could feel only a tiny trickle of pulse. I passed my hand up to his head. The cap was gone and the hair was stiff and matted with frozen blood, but just above the ear I felt a warm moist spot. I knew that this was the wounded point and that the fresh blood was oozing forth. The bullet had entered the brain and the soldier was unconscious, but it was evidently the man whose cap the dog had brought to our trenches.

One of the orderlies had a first aid kit, and we hurriedly put on a dressing to keep the dirt out. We slid him on to the stretcher and started back, crawling and dragging the stretcher after us.

Our progress was necessarily very slow, for with each rocket we had to lie quiet. The German trenches were not more than forty yards away. Finally, however, we reached our wire and passed through one of the lanes which had been cut to let the attacking waves through.

The stretcher was carefully passed down to waiting hands below, and the wounded man wrapped in blankets, and we started back for the dressing station.

I learned that the other two dogs had returned in the meantime, one with a cap and the other with a piece of cloth ripped by his fangs from a wounded man's overcoat. The dogs are trained to tear something from the soldier's garments if they cannot find a cap or glove. Whatever the dog brings back is used to refresh its memory when the rescue party starts after the wounded man, the orderly passing it across the animal's nose whenever he falters.

One of the rescue parties returned with an abdominal case, a bad one, so weak that I could scarcely detect a sign of life.

"Do the dogs ever take you to dead bodies?" I asked the orderly.

"No, Excellency, never," he replied. "They sometimes lead us to bodies which we think have no life in them, but when we bring them back the doctors, by careful examination, always find a spark though often very feeble. It is purely a matter of instinct, which, in this instance, is far more effective than man's reasoning powers."

Presently a third party returned with a man with a broken thigh. He was almost lifeless from exposure and shock.

So the work went on until we had recovered fourteen wounded. Then one of the dogs returned without anything in his mouth. He was sent back again and while he was gone another returned, also without any "evidence." When, after a little while, all three dogs stuck their shaggy heads over the parapet with nothing in their mouths we were tolerably sure that there were no more wounded Russians in the thicket.

By that time the first gray light of dawn was struggling to dispel the night. As I went back to the main dressing station through the ghostly forest, our artillery was pounding furiously at the German lines. Then came the infernal crackle of rifles and the *tack! tack!* of machine-guns and the flickering of rockets as another wave of our infantry went over the top in a second desperate attack to break the German lines. As I pictured the inrush of the flowing stream of wounded pouring down the road through the forest to our dressing stations, I realized that there would be little rest for me that day.

Chapter XV
SOUND SLEEPERS

Events of that day are blurred in my mind. I was so tired that the only impression I retained was of an apparently endless round of work. Wounded, wounded; and then more wounded! I have a dim picture of them lying patiently in the tent, which was soon overflowing, and a perfect sea of them in the wet snow outside. It was a case of plodding through operations with dogged perseverance—here a hurried amputation, there a brain operation or an abdominal section—on and on without end. In a night's work of that description, a man performs more operations and treats more cases than the busiest practitioner sees in a month of private practice, and while conditions work havoc with technique, such an experience is a wonderful developer of resourcefulness. I remember hearing the same contradictory accounts of how our attack was faring through the early morning mists and of the final authoritative news that we had failed again and, after sustaining frightful losses, had been forced to give up the German first-line in the face of stiff counterattack.

Toward late afternoon we had most of the wounded attended to. Our poor ambulance horses were ready to drop. They had been going continuously for twenty-four hours.[1]

The old Colonel of the artillery dropped in to see how we were faring. His fur-coat looked like the top of a pepper-box where it was shot full of holes from the fragments of an H E shell. The thick leather had checked the force of the little pieces of steel and they had scarcely gone through his inside clothing.

"No, it didn't hurt me," the old fellow yelled, in answer to my inquiry, "but it killed one of my cows, damn them!" The curse evidently referred to the Germans, not to the cows, for the loss of the one was a sad blow to the Colonel—so much so, indeed, that he mentioned only incidentally, as he left to go back to his battery, that the same shell had accounted for ten of his men—four killed and six wounded!

"I'll pound them to pieces tonight!" he yelled.

"The damned Nemets—I'll pound them to pieces!"

His battery certainly made enough noise to pound anything to pieces, and I knew it was no use trying to get any sleep in that vicinity that night. As evening ap-

---

[1] Medical workers at the front often worked long shifts, sometimes more than 24–48 hours without rest.

proached, therefore, and the last of the wounded had started on his journey to the divisional hospital, I walked back to a group of deserted houses that I knew of, leaving word with Mike to call for me if a third attack started or more wounded arrived.

I took a blanket with me, as it promised to be cold sleeping in an uninhabited house. It was just getting dark when I approached the peasant's cottage near which stood a barn and several small outhouses. The cottage had been partly wrecked by a German shell and the thatched roof was caved in and all the windows were broken by the explosion. It was very desolate looking and gloomy, but at any rate the noise was not so had and I figured I could get some sleep.

The barn looked a little better than the house, and I thought I would take a look at it. I opened the low door and peered into what had formerly been a storeroom for tools and farming utensils. It was quite dark in there. The odor of old straw assailed my nostrils. As I stepped in, my foot sunk in a bed of dry chaff, and it seemed like a good place to sleep after all.

As my eyes became accustomed to the gloom, I noticed a number of soldiers stretched out on the straw. There were eight or ten of them lying about in the postures that men assume when thoroughly exhausted. They had thrown themselves down to snatch a few hours' sleep. l figured that they were too tired to be easily awakened, but l picked my way quietly between them, treading softly on the yielding straw and selecting an unoccupied spot between two of the slumbering forms, I stretched out, rolled myself up in my blanket and was soon sound asleep; the enormous amount of work and the excitement of the last few days, combined with the lack of sleep, had left me pretty well exhausted, and I think l would have slept for the next twenty-four hours at least if I had not been awakened—perhaps an hour after I had lain down—by a terrific crash—the smashing detonation of a shell close to the barn.

I lay listening, startled by the explosion, and was just falling to sleep again when a second shell came screeching down and another crash shook the old barn. I wondered what would happen to us all if the Germans dropped a shell right on the ham, and just then a third shell exploded and I was covered with a shower of dirt and straw, a large hole appearing in the roof of the barn at the farthermost end where the shell had scraped the thatch of the roof off as it flew over and hit in the field beyond.

Strangely enough, the explosions had not awakened the others or, if they had, they had fallen off to sleep again at-once.

It occurred to me, however, that the Germans were now firing directly at the barn, probably figuring that it was occupied by reserves, and that the next shell would probably finish all of us, and I decided that I would clear out.

"We had better get out of here!" I yelled in Russian.

The soldiers didn't budge.

"Come on, now!" I repeated. "Wake up, Galoopchicks; we've got to get out of here!" And I reached out and clutched the one nearest me by the coat and shook him and shouted in his ear. Still he didn't budge.

A startling truth began to dawn on my drowsy senses. I felt in my pocket for my electric torch and flashed its white beam on him. His face was the color of ashes, his eyes stared at me with a fishy stare, his lips were drawn in an awful grin, he was dead! I turned the light on the others—dead! Every one stark dead! My companions were corpses—I was sleeping in a mortuary!

I could feel my hair bristle, and a cold chill ran down my spine, as I jumped up, leaped over several still forms, and bolted for the door.

As I scurried away, I heard again the moaning call approaching nearer and nearer out of the inky sky. I crouched low as it crashed and looked back over my shoulder. The old barn was lit up by a hellish glare which revealed a whirling mass of boards and smoke as it flew apart like a pack of cards. The last shell had been a clean hit, right into the center of the old structure—in the room of the dead.

I hurried back to the dressing station, stumbling along through the gloomy pine forest to the road. The shouting of the drivers of some artillery limbers, loaded with shells, which came clanking down the road, was pleasant music to my ears.

When I arrived at the tent Michael asked me if it had been too cold to sleep in the old house, and I told him of my silent companions.

"They were probably placed there until tomorrow when they were to be buried," he explained. "Meester sleep here in the tent and if the wounded come I shall call him."

I lay down on my blankets and fell sound asleep once more. I did not wake until morning. When I opened my eyes, I noticed several fresh jagged holes in the tent and asked Mike about them.

"Two shells hit close to the tent last night," he replied; "but you were asleep and I didn't call you, as no more came."

During the morning Colonel Starik called and told me I had better move the dressing station back half a mile, as he considered it very dangerous to remain where we were.

To have moved back, however, would have made it necessary for the wounded and our stretcher-bearers to walk just so much farther and we decided to stay where we were. Later I was to learn how much wiser it would have been to have heeded the Colonel's warning.

The Colonel was very much discouraged as to the outcome of this battle.

"We shall probably attack again tonight," he said. "We'll have more reserves up then. There will be some further artillery preparation, but I think it very foolish to continue. They are fully prepared for us and I don't think we have a chance of breaking through. I've lost over two-thirds of my regiment!"

Lieutenant Muhanoff dropped in a little later. His regiment was so depleted that it had been sent into reserve, and the Lieutenant had plenty of time at his command. I was glad that he was out of it, temporarily at any rate, as I was becoming very fond of him.

"Isn't it wonderful how our soldiers go into the attack again and again without flinching?" he asked, admiringly. "Each new regiment that comes up knows, of course, of the enormous losses of the one whose place they are taking, and yet they enter the fight with the utmost bravery.[2] As I came up the road I passed our fifth regiment going into reserve, and I don't believe there was one thousand men left out of the original four thousand."

I could but agree with him, for I had learned to respect these sturdy peasant soldiers.

Late in the afternoon a German plane soared over our trenches, high up in the blue sky, accompanied on its course by the cotton-like puffs of shrapnel from our anti-aircraft guns. The far-off drone of his motor could be heard as he circled about, dropping slightly near the earth as he passed directly over our tent.

I wondered if he could make us out nestling down there among the pines or if he could see through our pine bough camouflage.

I retired early that night, for there would probably be an attack at daybreak and I would have to be about early to prepare for the new crop of wounded. Sometime in the night I heard our artillery open up an intense fire, but dropped off to sleep again despite the noise, and with never an inkling of what was in store for me on the morrow.

---

[2] The notion that Russian soldiers were unwaveringly brave and dedicated to the cause of the war was commonly held and expressed by pro-war public opinion, especially the elite. In reality, most peasant soldiers were not enthusiastic about the war, the aims of which they little understood or identified with, and instead, went to battle with what Allan Wildman has described as "sullen resignation" to a fate they believed was beyond their control. See Allan Wildman, *The End of the Russian Imperial Army: The Old Army and the Soldiers' Revolt (March–April 1917)* (Princeton: Princeton University Press, 1980), as well as Nicholas Golovin, *The Russian Army in the World War* (New Haven: Yale University Press, 1931), and Joshua A. Sanborn, *Drafting the Russian Nation: Military Conscription, Total War, and Mass Politics, 1905–1925* (DeKalb: Northern Illinois University Press, 2003).

Chapter XVI
INJURED BY A SHELL

I was awakened by Mike shaking me and shouting in my ear.

"Quick, Meester, to the *blindage* (bomb-proof)!" he was yelling excitedly. "German shoot 'em up like hell!"

They surely were shooting us up! I could hear the distant roar of their artillery, with the peculiar double reports *loom-boom* blurred into a constant roll of drum-fire. Their shells were literally sweeping the forest. A constant stream was pouring in, whistling and crashing, and I could hear their fragments buzzing through the air like a swarm of angry bees, and the sound of falling limbs and branches. Several pieces struck the tent, ripping through the canvas and leaving jagged holes.

I jumped up and followed Mike out of the tent and we plunged through the darkness for a little bomb-proof which my orderlies had dug in the sodden ground near the tent.

It was a tiny affair about five feet square and about four feet deep. It had a fairly strong roof of logs and dirt but it was half full of melted snow-water.

"Come, Meester, come quick!" shouted Mike above the uproar, as we heard the wail of another shell coming down. I figured that it would be very close this time as I leaped over a dead horse and made for the sound of Mike's voice in the darkness ahead.

There was a terrific blinding flash right at my side, and I knew no more.

The first sensation I had on recovering consciousness was a sharp pain in my head, and the second of being in icy water up to my waist, but the third and most startling thing was the absolute stillness.

I looked about me. Above, not a foot from my face, were a number of logs placed close together. Then I saw a hand holding a candle and then Mike's face, as white as chalk, peering down at me, with tears streaming from his eyes.

I put out my hand, groping about, and came in contact with icy water, which covered the lower part of my body. Then I realized that I was in the little bomb-proof and that Mike was holding me up, keeping my face and chest out of the water with one hand and holding the lighted candle with his other.

His lips moved but I heard no sound, neither could I hear the artillery—it was silent as a tomb.

I wondered why it was so still, for I recalled the noise of an instant before.

I spoke to Mike, asking him if they had stopped shelling us—and I could not hear my own voice!

Apparently I was stone-deaf! I put my fingers in my ears and they came away slightly blood stained. Then I realized that the explosion had broken my ear-drums.

Mike started to crawl out of the bomb-proof, dragging me with him, but I told him I was quite able to walk, and when I got out I stood up unassisted, feeling only a little weak. There was a slight buzzing in my ears.

When we got back to our tent, I noticed that there were several small tears in my coat just over the left chest and then I felt a stinging sensation at this point. Examination revealed several small fragments of steel imbedded in the skin which Mike pulled out with forceps, touching the bleeding points with iodine.

Dawn was showing its first gray light by this time and I decided to visit the scene of the explosion which had felled me. A big tree lying on the ground at this point told me the story.

The shell had come directly toward me but had struck the tree five feet above the ground. It had exploded where it struck, cutting the tree entirely off at this point, which was about twenty inches in diameter. The tree had toppled over but the force of the shell had carried the trunk forward toward me, the top falling in the opposite direction. I had been about four feet from the tree when the shell struck and the force of the explosion had hurled me to the ground. The fragments, coming through twenty inches of tough green wood, had lost their velocity and did not have force enough to go through my skin.

Had I been out of line of the tree I would no doubt have been killed instantly. As it was, the only injury I suffered was the rupturing of my ear-drums and the condition known as shell-shock[1] due to dynamic air pressure, which sometimes amounts to as much as ten tons to the square yard in the vicinity of a large shell when it explodes.

I had seen many cases of ruptured ear-drums and knew that they all healed up and hearing was fully restored within two or three weeks, so I considered myself very lucky.

When I recovered my hearing some two weeks later, Mike told me his part of the story.

He had been some thirty feet in front of me, ready to dive into the bomb-proof, when he heard the shell coming. He called to me to hurry and jumped into the bomb-proof just as the shell exploded. When I did not arrive, he concluded I had been killed or wounded and came to look for me. Shells were breaking all about, but he ran to where I had been and found me lying close to the dead horse. Then he had dragged me back to the bomb-proof through a perfect hail of flying fragments and had suc-

---

[1] This is a strange and somewhat inaccurate use of the term "shell shock." Most often it referred to what is now termed "post-traumatic stress disorder"—psychological strain as a result of exposure to war. The term "shell shock" was actually coined during the First World War.

ceeded in getting me inside, holding my face above the water which was a foot deep, while he contrived to light a candle with the other hand.

Although he could not find any wounds by the light of the candle, he thought I was dead. Most of the Russian orderlies become greatly attached to the officers they serve and Mike was not an exception in this case: hence the tear-stained face which I saw when I opened my eyes. He was a brave, faithful fellow, and I probably owe my life to his devotion, for if he had allowed me to lie where I had fallen, I should undoubtedly have been struck by pieces of shells, several of which landed close by.

The following day I decided to follow the suggestion the Colonel had made and move my dressing station a half mile back. The aeroplane which had flown over the day before had possibly spotted our tent and the German artillery might give us another bombardment any moment—perhaps worse than the one we had gone through.

While we were packing up, I received word from Colonel Kalpaschnecoff that our division was to go into reserve and that we should move back to our base in the village about eight miles from the line.

Our division had lost over one-half its men and was unable to continue the offensive. It would be replaced by one of the divisions in reserve, drawn from one of the five army corps commanded by General Pleschcoff.[2]

I was glad that there was to be no more work, for my head was bothering me a great deal and it was difficult to "carry on" on account of my absolute deafness.

Late in the afternoon we started with our long line of ambulances and transports, hoping to cross the exposed road in the dusk of the evening when the German observers would be unable to make us out.

The day had been warm and sunny and had converted the road into rivers of mud and snow water up to the hubs of the ambulances. The setting sun cast its long rays over the marshes and flooded fields and there was a feeling of spring in the air. A flock of wild geese went honking far overhead, winging their way steadily northward.

When we passed the group of deserted houses where I had slept with my silent companions two nights before, I saw that a shell had completely demolished the old barn and that only a tumbled mass of boards and rafters remained.

The roadside was dotted with little crosses erected over the graves of soldiers who had died of their wounds en route to the divisional hospital, for we were jolting down the same road we had sent the wounded over.

The roads were blocked with limbers loaded with shells to feed the guns; the horses straining at the traces knee-deep in mud and water, trying to pull the heavy carts, the drivers yelling and flying the whip, and our progress was slow.

As evening approached we crossed the open field where we had been shelled coming in and saw dozens of horses sprawled out along the roadside. We passed one

---

[2] Pleshkov was in command of all of the forces in the northern portion of the front, which actually only included four army corps in addition to the 1st Siberian Army Corps: the I and XXVII Army Corps, and the VII Cavalry Corps.

of our battalions silently splashing through the icy water, tired and bedraggled from three days of constant fighting, their faces white and drawn as they trudged back to the reserve billets. They did not march in order but in a straggling line, picking their way through the water-covered fields to avoid the mud of the road, and there was not three hundred of the original twelve hundred left!

Just before we entered the forest beyond the field, I turned in my saddle and looked back toward the positions for the last time.

Another bombardment was on, and while I could not hear it, I could feel the heavy air vibrations as it rolled in drum-fire, and could see the rockets rise, flickering over the dark forest which lay between. A gray haze of smoke stretched above the tree-tops, dimly visible in the fast fading light, marking the barrage.

I turned, and touching my horse lightly with my spurs, passed into the forest, the trees shutting off my last view of that great battle. It ended in failure so far as advancing our lines was concerned, but it served to divert a great number of German troops from our hard-pressed French allies at Verdun—and perhaps that achievement was worth all it cost.[3] In that battle we lost half of our army corps of 50,000 men; and other corps which were engaged before it was over—it lasted several days after I left—also lost heavily.[4] On our side there were thirteen attacks of importance. It required men with nerves of steel to charge across that hell of No Man's Land, but those Russian peasant soldiers did it time after time. They realized that it was almost sure death to do so, but there was no flinching. Many were killed in the reserve positions without even a rifle in their hands; for because of the machinations of pro-German plotters in Petrograd our troops never had sufficient rifles.[5] Many times they had to wait until rifles taken from the wounded could be given to them. There is nothing which will break the morale of troops so quickly as to be under shell fire without a weapon of defense in their hands. Then, too, the knowledge that they had been betrayed to the Germans, that they had known for weeks before of our plans and had concentrated such an overwhelming amount of guns and men at this point to break down our attacks, had a most depressing effect. The wonder of it was that our troops attacked at all in the face of such discouragement.

---

[3] In fact, the attack had been launched at the request of the French with the intention of relieving German pressure on their troops on the Western Front.

[4] Pleshkov's combined forces (4 corps) sustained casualties of more than 48,000, over 50% of the original number of troops. In all, the Russians lost over 78,000 troops, comprising 30% of the forces that had gone to battle. See Podorozhnyi, *Narochskaia operatsiia*, 150.

[5] By this time in the war, Russian production of armaments, including rifles, had improved considerably, so serious shortages were no longer a problem. Moreover, earlier shortages were the result of insufficient planning and lack of competency in coordination and distribution rather than sabotage.

Chapter XVII
THE MEDAL OF ST. GEORGE

Back in the peaceful little village, with straw-thatched cabins, the sounds of the bitter fighting raging in the forest and swamps along the front came to us like distant thunder. The village was a perfect haven of rest to our fagged brains, worn almost to the breaking-point by the excitement and nervous strain of the past week.

The spring was just beginning to dispel the long stern winter and the smell of fresh earth and new budding life was in the air. The sound of running water told us that the iron fetters of the Frost King had been broken.

My hearing gradually came back and the noises in my head cleared up, but I was still nervous from the shock of the exploding shell.

One day Colonel Kalpaschnecoff came to me and with a twinkle in his brown eyes, said: "A personage, one of the Grand Dukes, is coming to our corps bearing the personal thanks of the Emperor to the soldiers and officers of the First Siberian Army Corps for their valiant efforts in the fighting of last week. I was ordered by General Pleschcoff to tell you that your presence would be required on the field when the troops are reviewed by His High Excellency, the Grand Duke."

"What has that got to do with me?" I asked in astonishment.

"I presume General Pleschcoff desires your presence to lend éclat to the occasion," he replied, smiling. "Anyway, be sure to be on hand, dress up in your best duds, and don't forget it's scheduled for the day after tomorrow at 2:30 P.M."

I went to the review and stood with the officers of the staff, and heard the High Personage speak a few words of praise to our men, who were drawn up in a great hollow square. The regiments were dwindled to a mere handful of their former numbers, and some companies had no officers at all to command the thirty or forty survivors—companies which had numbered two hundred men two weeks before.

Certain soldiers were called by name and stepped out of line, advanced to the center of the field, and stood at attention before the Personage.

Medals and crosses, dangling from ribbons of orange and black, were pinned to their left breasts over the heart.

More kind words were spoken by the Personage and General Pleschcoff, and then the soldiers saluted, wheeled, and marched stiffly back into the ranks.

Certain officers were then called by name and stepped into the field, where little white crosses suspended from orange and black ribbons were similarly pinned to their breasts.

Among the names called was a strangely foreign one and I felt the Colonel push me forward and say: "Hurry! That's you! Don't forget to salute with the right hand!"

So I walked out and stood at attention and the Personage smiled and said:

"Malcom Alvaovitch Grow, you have been mentioned by the commander of the first division in despatches to our Emperor. These despatches told how you stuck to your post through most trying circumstances, caring for our wounded Russians, although warned by Colonel Starik to retire, and how you set for your orderlies and for our soldiers an example of devotion to duty and bravery. For this the Emperor desires that I thank you and present to you the medal of St. George."

Then he pinned the medal on my left breast and kissed me on both cheeks, as did General Pleschcoff.[1]

I was too astonished to struggle, as would have become a true American, and I don't remember saluting, but the Colonel told me afterward that I did. As I walked off the field I heard dimly a roaring sound which I took to be the cheering of a large number of men, but I am not sure, for my hearing had not quite returned.

When I got back to where the officers were grouped I had to endure some more kissing by various bearded individuals.

A few days later Colonel Kalpaschnecoff asked me if I would like to go to America for a short leave of absence.

"You have been pretty well knocked about by that shell," he argued, "and the muddy season is at hand. The corps has lost half its men and won't be able to fight again for at least two months. We'll stay in reserve, filling up the gaps in the ranks for that length of time anyway, and I see no reason why you should not go."

I didn't either, and I hastily packed up and started for Petrograd.

I left our village at ten o'clock at night, riding the twenty versts to the station on horseback and there collecting my luggage which had been sent ahead by cart.

The Easter holidays were approaching and the trains were crowded with officers going home to celebrate the greatest of Russian holidays with their friends and families.

Many soldiers had also been given a furlough, and the third and fourth class waiting-room was crowded with soldiers sleeping on the floor and packed so tightly that one could scarcely walk. The first and second class waiting-room was nearly as congested, although the officers did not sleep on the floors.

The train was so crowded that we had to stand in the aisles. I stood for seventeen hours in all, sleeping part of the time as I stood. After a journey of several days,

---

[1] Kissing on both cheeks is a traditional form of greeting and congratulations in Russian culture.

during part of which, of course, I managed to get a seat, I finally came to Petrograd. There I had to wait eight days before I succeeded in getting permission to leave the country. My trip through Finland, Norway and Sweden to Christiana[2] where I took passage for America was without special incident.

I spent three delightful weeks in my own country and returned to Russia via Archangel,[3] arriving at that port in early June, 1916.

---

[2] In Denmark.

[3] Archangelsk, located in northern Russia on the White Sea.

Chapter XVIII
A DEMONSTRATION ATTACK

As we reached the entrance of the White Sea, we received reports of the Austrian concentration on the Italian front, how they had advanced to the edge of the plains and how Brusiloff's smashing drive[1] into Austria through Galicia and the Carpathians, with the capture of large numbers of prisoners, had caused such pressure on Austria that she had been obliged to withdraw her divisions from the Italian front and send them north against the Russians. This released the pressure in Italy and gave her time to bring up troops and stem the Austrian advance.

I felt sure that my corps would get into this action,[2] and I was anxious to rejoin it. I lost no time in getting to Petrograd, therefore, and after interviewing the commandant of the railroad station there I was able to secure a place-card for a berth on the train going to the front with very little delay.

At the little station ten miles back of the line where our troops were in the trenches south of Lake ———,[3] I was met by the old victoria driven by Michael, my orderly.

He was overjoyed at seeing me back and inquired if my hearing had been completely restored after the shell shock.

"I think we'll have a big fight in a few days," he said.

---

[1] The Brusilov Offensive—named for the commander who planned and led it, General Aleksei Brusilov—was a major push undertaken by the Russian army beginning on June 4 and lasting until August 10, 1915. It was carried against the Austro-Hungarian armies and made use of small, specialized units known as "shock troops" that led the attacks. The attack was initially successful and allowed Russia to break through the Austrian lines. It also forced the Germans to halt their offensive against Verdun and transfer troops to shore up the faltering Austrian forces. In the end, however, it left both sides significantly damaged, having incurred heavy losses (more than 2 million Russian and 1.5 million Austro-Hungarian troops killed, wounded, or captured). For more, see Timothy Dowling, *The Brusilov Offensive* (Bloomington: Indiana University Press, 2008), as well as D. Stone, *The Russian Army in the Great War*. For Brusilov's own account, see Aleksei A. Brusilov, *A Soldier's Note-book, 1914–1918* (London: Macmillan, 1930).

[2] When Grow rejoined it in June 1916, the 1st Siberian was with the Second Army on the Western Front, north of where the Brusilov Offensive had begun (on the Southwestern Front), Later, in July, it was transferred to the Special Army to join the offensive.

[3] This is likely Lake Naroch, north of the Belorussian city of Minsk and east of the Lithuanian city Vilnius.

I could hear the artillery booming in steady drum-fire in the positions twenty miles away to the west.

The roads, now dry and in good condition, were filled with transport wagons hauling supplies to the troops. I was struck by the number of little colts which trotted along on their stiltlike legs beside their mothers who pulled at the shafts of the heavy carts. They were nearly all the same size and age—born in the spring of the year. Some of the very youngest were so weak that the kindly drivers, seeing they had grown tired, had lifted them up in the carts and they were riding along, gazing out over the side with their great dark eyes, apparently quite content.

Nearly every cart had one of these youngsters either riding in the box or running alongside.

When they reach a sufficient age they are sent to great breeding stations, where they are reared and broken to harness or used for cavalry horses. The Russians had ten million horses at the outbreak of the war, but at the end of two years of warfare this number had been sadly depleted and every effort was being made to increase it.

Our base was in a little village four miles back of the lines, in a house belonging to the village priest. As soon as I arrived we dined out of doors beneath a great vine which climbed over a lattice work.

While we were seated at dinner a German plane flew over. Our anti-aircraft guns were firing at it and their tiny white puffs of shrapnel dotted the sky overhead, eight thousand feet in the air. Suddenly we heard a *whir-r-r-r-r* from above, which became louder as it approached. We thought the German had dropped a bomb and we waited tensely for the explosion.

The priest sat directly opposite me and as I glanced at him I was struck at the set expression of his face and the deathly pallor. He held a fork poised in his hand, half-way to his mouth.

The missile landed with a loud thud not four feet back of my chair, knocking leaves from the branches overhead on to our tablecloth. The priest's fork clattered to the table, he bowed his head and crossed himself three times. A longdrawn sigh of relief escaped my lips and I got up to examine the object which had so narrowly missed me.

I found a neat circular hole in the earth about three and a half inches in diameter.

"Be careful!" Colonel Kalpaschnecoff warned, as I cautiously reached down. "If it is a defective bomb, the slightest jar may cause it to explode!" I reached down until my arm was in above the elbow, when I felt a metallic disk which I recognized to be the rear end of a shrapnel casing. After some difficulty I managed to lift it out and found that it was an empty casing, one which had been fired by our own guns, had discharged its pellets at the Boche when its time fuse ignited the powder charge, and had then fallen to the earth. The dropping of these shrapnel cases is the cause of many casualties. They drop from a height of five or six thousand feet and naturally attain tremendous velocity. I attended a soldier who had been struck on the foot by one of them, completely amputating that member at the instep. Another poor fellow was hit directly on the head and killed outright, his skull being crushed like an eggshell.

"The Germans are sending their greeting to you on your arrival from America," remarked the Colonel, as we resumed our meal, and I kept the empty shell-casing as a souvenir of my return to the Russian army. It weighs about ten pounds and serves as a receptacle for flowers.

"We will have a demonstration attack in a few days," the Colonel enlightened me, when the tea was served and we had lighted our cigarettes. "The object of the action will be to prevent the Germans from sending troops to the south to reinforce the hard-pressed Austrians where Brusiloff is driving them steadily back, taking large numbers of prisoners.

"At the same time that we attack, there will be a great offensive about a hundred miles south of us at Baranovitchi. Our corps will not attempt to pierce the German line. In fact, if we capture their first and second lines we shall occupy them only a short time and then return to our own lines."

The next morning I rode out to our main dressing station, which was located in a peasant's cottage about one verst (five-eighths of a mile) back of the trenches. The house belonged to a man about seventy years of age, and despite the shelling the place had received, the old fellow wouldn't leave.

He was the only peasant remaining in the locality, all the inhabitants of the neighboring village having fled when the Germans approached. As he tended to his bees, of which he had about twenty hives, he reminded me very much of Tolstoy,[4] whom he strongly resembled.

We used the large room of the house for our dressing station, and we fixed up an old barn to serve as an annex where the wounded might be placed while waiting for the ambulances to remove them to the division hospital.

There was not sufficient time to make a bombproof, so I pitched a little tent under an apple tree in the garden where it was well screened from German observers by the foliage. About fifty feet from the tent a line of well-constructed reserve trenches cut diagonally across the garden, and they could be used as a refuge in case of heavy shelling.

I ate my meals in the open on a box placed under the apple-tree, as my tent was thickly infested with flies. By closing the flap of the tent during meals I was able to pen them in and could eat my food in comparative peace.

The German positions were on a ridge about a verst away from my tent and in plain view as I sat at my meals.

Our artillery, which was back of me firing over my head, was pouring a steady rain of projectiles on the ridge, and fifteen or twenty shells could be seen bursting at

---

[4] Lev Tolstoy, famed Russian writer; author of *War and Peace*, *Anna Karenina*, among other classics; considered by some to be Russia's, if not the world's, greatest writer. He was known for advocating for a simple, peasant lifestyle, and often spent his time working the land on his estate.

one time on the skyline. The constant stream of shells striking the ridge at various points along the crest threw up fountains of black smoke and dirt to a height of a hundred feet and more, looking like strange trees which developed as you watched.

Lieutenant Muhanoff dropped in for dinner the afternoon that I arrived and we were sitting watching the shelling while Michael served dinner.

Several German shells came moaning toward our batteries, which were situated in the wood back of us about five hundred yards from the garden.

We had finished dinner and were sitting enjoying the fine warm sunshine when Michael, who was standing nearby, held up his hand and cried. "Listen!"

Whoo! We heard the shell coming and all three dived for the shelter of the reserve-trench, which was only a few steps from where we sat. We had barely jumped in before the shell exploded with a frightful crash just back of the tent in the middle of the garden.

We crouched down in the bottom of the trench waiting for the next one, which came over presently and burst near the house.

Just as it exploded, Michael, who was sitting on the fire-step of the trench, clapped his hand to his forehead with a loud cry. I decided that he had been struck by a piece of shell and stepped over to him. He was holding his hand to his forehead and his face was ghastly.

No blood appeared between his fingers.

"Do you think I am done for?" he whispered, as I removed his hands.

All I could see was a little red spot just above the eyebrow, in the center of which was stuck a black spine like a small thorn.

He was terribly frightened and I was just about to assure him that whatever it was it would not prove fatal, when something hit me in back of the neck with such force that my head rocked.

A terrible burning followed, and immediately afterward I received a second blow on the left cheek, followed by a similar smarting burn.

There was a startled cry from the Lieutenant, and he started running up the trench, wildly beating the air with his hands.

When a third shell came whistling in and exploded, Michael gave vent to a howl and jumped up, shouting: "The bees! The bees!"

The air was now full of an angry humming, and as I started off in full flight after Michael, who was now following the Lieutenant, I received another lightning stab on the back of the neck.

The shells landing among the dozen or more hives had by the force of their explosion knocked them over, and the little owners, furious at this disturbance, had gone forth to give battle. We were the innocent victims of their attack.

A perfect swarm of the angry insects buzzed about my head as I ran, fanning the air with both hands. The Lieutenant, unable to make sufficient headway in the narrow crooked trench, threw discretion to the winds, leaped the parapet, and ran madly across the field, away from the garden. Michael, his head surrounded by a cloud of convoys, followed suit, but not being so agile as the Lieutenant, stumbled and fell rolling down the parapet into the field.

Another shell came screeching in and hit on the edge of the garden, and the air was full of the buzzing of a more destructive agent than our tormentors, the bees.

Michael, alarmed at the proximity of the shell-burst, leaped to his feet and dashed off, fear and pain giving added speed to his flight.

I decided the bees were preferable to the shells, and seeing the door of the bomb-proof open I ran into the sheltering gloom of the interior, where I brushed off two or three bees who were clinging to my clothes. I stayed in the bomb-proof until the Germans had ceased shelling, and then went in search of the other victims.

I had completely lost the vision of one eye from an enormous swelling which closed it tight, but I succeeded in finding the Lieutenant and Michael. They were seated on the grass at the farther end of the field and presented a wonderful spectacle with their swollen features.

As the Lieutenant rose to go he told me that his company was not going over in the attack scheduled for the following night.

"I know of an observation point from which we can see the beginning of the fight," he said, "and if you care to, come to my regiment tomorrow afternoon and we'll watch it together."

I promised to do so provided I could get back to the dressing station in time to attend the wounded when they came in.

"Very well," he said; "you can leave right after the first wave goes over."

Our artillery kept up a steady systematic fire all night and the next day. In the afternoon I rode to where the Lieutenant's regiment was billeted in dug-outs in the forest in reserve. I left my horse there and we walked a mile to the positions where they ran along on the top of some high sand ridges.

We went through an approach-trench which zigzagged up one of these hills, the highest of the series. At the very top was built a strong bombproof which was used as an observation point.

Just over the brow of the hill were our first line trenches which faced the Germans on a series of lower ridges about three hundred yards away, a shallow ravine lying between.

Far off on the right flank, stretching away for miles to the horizon, were the blue waters of Lake ———,[5] part of which was in German hands and part in ours.

The right flank of our corps rested on the edge of the lake; and across six miles of intervening water I could see, through the periscope in the observation point, the yellow lines of the trenches begin on its farther shore, which was held by another corps.

---

[5] Lake Naroch, around which the previous failed offensive had taken place, was directly on the front line separating German and Russian territory.

As it grew dusky and our artillery increased its fire, the Germans kept their rockets flying in the air in expectation of an attack. By 12:30 A.M., when our troops went over the top, the German line simply spouted rockets until it looked like a fireworks exhibition at Coney Island. There were white ones by the thousand and dozens of red ones—the latter being used where our troops were pressing the Germans hard and they wanted a more intense artillery barrage.

During early July in this part of Russia the nights are never entirely dark, but the field was covered by a pall of smoke through which could be seen the angry red bursts of shrapnel like lightning through a cloud mass on a summer night. By the light of these shrapnel explosions and the white, red, and green flares of the enemy's rockets, we could see the entire line of attack, which was over a front of one kilometer.

The crackle of the machine-guns and rifles was intense at first but gradually quieted down. That was a good sign, for it indicated that our men had taken the first two lines and had silenced the German gunners.

I was loath to leave the wonderful sight, but I knew the wounded were starting to pour back through the communication-trenches and I had to hurry back to my dressing station.

As I hurried through a communication-trench I passed dozens of wounded, who were slowly wending their way back, many sitting down to rest for a few moments to recover from the pain and shock of their wounds.

At our advanced dressing station, which was in a strong dug-out under the lea of a sand-hill, I stopped a moment to see how the students Metia and Nicholi were coming on with the work.

The dug-out was packed with wounded and dozens were lying on the ground outside patiently waiting their turn. The students, whose white gowns were splattered with blood, were working like mad in the dull light of a couple of candles.

I hurried on across some low-lying ground studded with little pine-trees, toward the main dressing room in the old peasant's house. On a narrow trail were dozens of parties of stretcher bearers, four to a stretcher, stumbling along through the semi-darkness bearing their moaning, pain-stricken burdens, while other wounded soldiers, barely able to walk, reeled along like drunken men, headed for our dressing station.

In the stress of battle we had to make men walk who were hideously wounded. I have seen them reel in with their jaws shot off, with both arms shot through, or with a gaping hole through the thigh. Sometimes a terribly wounded man would come in leading another who had been blinded in both eyes.

I soon outdistanced these crawling wretches and had a free path to the dressing station, where I found everything in readiness. The orderlies had sterilized my instruments, gauze and bandages were at hand, and the ambulances were drawn up in a long line waiting for their passengers.

Working steadily till ten o'clock the next morning, we handled two hundred and eighty wounded men that night in the little dressing station.

As we were finishing the bandaging of the last soldier, Lieutenant Muhanoff came into the bandage-strewn room and I asked him if the demonstration attack had been a success.

"Yes, yes, a great success," he replied. "As you know, our men only stayed a few minutes in the German trenches after taking the first two lines. They didn't intend to. It was not a serious attempt to pierce the lines. We lost about three thousand men in killed and wounded out of the three regiments which attacked."

"Three thousand men lost in a mere demonstration!" I exclaimed. "Wasn't that pretty costly work just to keep the Germans from shifting troops?"

"That is war," commented the Lieutenant, shrugging his shoulders. "I have seen in your America—what do you call it—ah, yes—the prizefight. In these contests I have seen one man pretend to strike his opponent and yet have no intention of doing so. It is what you call a feint, isn't it? Now that man may be very tired and the movement may cause him to use up some much needed energy, yet he must do it to deceive his opponent. It's general results which count. So it is with us—the real blow comes in the south but we must make a pretense of attacking here farther north in order to deceive the enemy. It costs some men, of course,—in other words, it uses up some of our energy—but the general staff have counted the cost and they decided that three thousand men was not too much to pay."

It was quite logical, of course, but none the less horrifying.

We walked out of the dingy little room into the warm morning sunshine where the birds were singing. The last of the ambulances was rattling off over the road in a cloud of dust. The artillery on both sides was silent and not a machine-gun or rifle could be heard on our sector of the front; but far off to the south could be heard a low muttering rumble.

"That's the battle of Baranovitchi," said the Lieutenant. "You can hear the guns although it is hundreds of miles away!"

I inhaled deep breaths of the sweet-scented air. The sunshine acted like a tonic after the long night's work, which seemed like the memory of a terrible dream.

We sat down to a cup of coffee under the spreading apple-tree and we could see the ridge on which the German trenches lay. Yesterday it had been a spouting mass of sand and smoke, but now it shimmered yellow, silent and deserted under the dancing heat rays.

The old peasant limped about in his bare feet, his loose white *rooboshka*[6] (shirt) flapping in the morning breeze, as he repaired the damage done by the German shells to his beehives.

---

[6] *Rubashka*.

Another scene of the great drama had finished, and except for a few more gaps in our brown-clad ranks and a few more crosses in a little cemetery, the world went on as before.

Chapter XIX
WE JOIN BRUSILOFF'S BIG DRIVE

After the demonstration attack, our corps was moved back near the railroad and billeted in little villages which were scattered over the surrounding territory.

The gaps in our ranks were rapidly filled up and in a week our corps received orders to be ready to entrain in four days.

Everyone knew we were going south somewhere, but to just what point on the line no one could be certain.

In the evening of the third day we moved our entire outfit to the station, camping that night in a grove of trees along the track.

The loading of 50,000 men, a division of artillery, a regiment of Cossacks, the staff and its equipment, to say nothing of the enormous number of little transport carts, with their horses, was a difficult task.

The railroad was a single-track affair, with only one siding. Nevertheless the trains, each of which consisted of thirty-five cars, pulled out with clocklike regularity.

We had an entire train for our ambulance column. Our ambulances were placed in flat cars, the horses led up planks into the box cars, six in each car, while the personnel occupied box cars fitted with tiers of rough planks at either end to sleep upon.

Russian troops are always moved in this fashion, the coaches being reserved for the officers. The Colonel, the students and I shared an old third-class car with some officers from the staff. We placed two field kitchens on a flat car and our food was cooked in them while travelling.

The trains followed each other in rapid succession, ours being in about the middle of the long line. Progress was slow and breakdowns were frequent.

At one point we burned out an axle bearing on one of the box cars. We stopped at a station and instead of cutting out this car, side-tracking it and substituting a new one, which could have been done in about ten minutes, they repaired the damaged one on the main track! An old bearded mechanic jacked up our car, seated himself on an old stool beside the axle, took out the burned-up bearing and, with a gouge, cut a new one out of some soft metal and fitted it to the axle. The operation took three hours and not only held us up for that length of time but also the twelve trains back of us.

After five days we reached Rovno[1] and detrained. The fighting unit of the corps went on by rail, as telegrams had been received from the corps whose places we were to take urging us to speed up as they had suffered such losses from German counter-attacks that they would be unable to hold out much longer. Because of lack of rail facilities, the transport and ambulance corps had to go to the fighting lines on their own wheels. Rovno was ninety miles from the trenches along the River Stockhod.[2]

After the fall of Warsaw, the Austro-German forces had advanced within twenty miles of Rovno, where, in September, 1915, the Russians had stemmed their advance. Both sides then entrenched and occupied the positions for nine months.

When Brusiloff started his big drive in June, 1916, the Austrians had been forced back with frightful losses until they had been able to check the Russian advances at the River Stockhod. The Russians had been pounding away at this line, trying to break through, for several weeks. If they could accomplish this, Kovel,[3] known as the "key of Warsaw," would be at their mercy.

Kovel was an important railway center, twenty miles beyond Stockhod River.

In August the Germans had rushed up many new divisions and were putting up a frightful defensive fight.

"Our corps has a difficult task to perform," said Colonel Kalpaschnecoff, as we rode along at the head of our long column of ambulances. "The Stockhod is a series of sluggish streams running through an immense marsh. We will be sent against the Prussian guard corps, which is defending the other bank of the river. It promises to be a terrible fight."

About eighteen miles from Rovno we came to the first of the old lines, which the Austrians had held since the fall of 1915 and had been forced out of early in August, just a few weeks before we arrived.

Where our road crossed the Russian trench line, we could see the signs of the intense fighting which had occurred there a short time before. The trenches were in a marshy field facing the Austrian lines, which ran along the border of a swampy forest.

The Russian trenches were of the built-up type, the ground being too marshy for deep digging. Sods of earth formed a high parapet, which had been badly battered by Austrian shell fire.

We crossed what had been No Man's Land and arrived at the abandoned Austrian trenches. They were beautifully constructed of great timbers, concrete and earth. In some places even steel rails had been cemented into place as protection against shell fire.

---

[1] Present-day Rivne, in western Ukraine.

[2] Stokhod (Stokhid, Ukrainian).

[3] Kovel'—city in northwestern Ukraine.

We dismounted to make a careful inspection of their construction. Near the road stood a large structure, with thick walls of logs and dirt. Apparently it had been an officer's bomb-proof.

As we tied our horses to a tree, an old peasant, leading a child by the hand, emerged from the door of the bomb-proof and approached us. Never have I seen a more forlorn spectacle than these two presented. The old man was in his bare feet, he was without a hat, his long gray hair falling in stringy unkempt masses over his shoulders, his frame was emaciated and bent, and his face had not known water for a long time. His clothes, mere rags, hung from his cadaverous frame like those of a scarecrow.

The child, too, presented a weird picture. It was a little boy about four years old, clad in a queer assortment of garments. On his head was a Russian soldier's cap, many sizes too large, falling down over his ears and half concealing his pinched, wan features. He wore an Austrian tunic, cast off by some soldier. It had once been gray but was now faded to an uncertain color. It had been made for a large man and descended well below the little fellow's knee, almost hiding the ragged homespun breeches he wore, while the sleeves dangled and flapped while he walked.

This strange pair came up to us, the old man bowing and peering out from under his shaggy, unkempt hair with the dull rheumy eyes of age. "Please, Excellencies," he said as he approached, "can you spare us a little bread? We have nothing to eat and are starving!"

The Colonel ordered one of the orderlies to bring some food. The fires in our field kitchens, which cook while on the march, were going, and the orderly came back with some steaming boiled beef, hot cassia, and black bread. He offered it to the old man and child. The youngster seized a piece of meat in his claw-like hands and proceeded to bolt it like a wild animal. The old man fell on his with equally ravenous energy.

"Have you seen my mama?" asked the little fellow, his eyes full of tears, after he had eaten all that he could. "She went away a long time ago and never came back!"

"Hush, dear!" the old man crooned. "Mama will come back to her baby in a few days." And then, turning to us, he added: "He asks that of all the soldiers who march by on the road. What can I do, Excellencies? We have no food, no home—only the mushrooms which I gather in the forest and what bread we can beg from the soldiers as they pass."

"Tell us what has happened," replied the Colonel. "Why do you live here in that bomb-proof?"

"It is a long story, Excellency."

"Never mind, tell us. We must stop here for lunch, and the horses must be fed and watered."

The old man seated himself at our feet and without further urging told us his story.

"My name is Gregory Paulovitch Arapoff. I lived in the village which you will pass if you follow that road. It is eight miles back of these trenches. I lived with my daughter, who is married and who is the mother of this little boy. She is twenty-four years old. Her husband is thirty eight. He had not been called to the colors when the Austrians came to our village last fall.

"We did not leave as some of the people did, for we were very poor and had only our cabin and what we could raise on a little patch of ground. Many Austrian soldiers and officers lived in our village from last summer up until a few weeks ago. We were ordered by the officers to keep three soldiers in the house. From time to time new soldiers came to live with us. We also had to give part of our potatoes and bread, milk from the cow, many chickens, and some of our pigs to the Austrians, but they always paid for them. They were not unkind to us, Excellency, but we never grew to like them."

The old man's arm stole around the little child, who had fallen asleep on the ground beside him. He pressed the tiny form to his sunken breast.

"No, they were not unkind to us at first," he continued. "One day early this summer the sound of the cannons increased in volume. Day and night we could hear the steady roar. Many wounded Austrians were brought to the hospital in the village.

"The road was filled with wagons, loaded with shells, and hundreds of soldiers. We were not allowed to leave the village during this time.

"One afternoon four soldiers and an under-officer came to the door of our cabin and asked my daughter and her husband to come to the house of the officer who had charge of the troops in the village. They called him the commandant. We thought they wished to buy more potatoes or bread. My daughter and her husband left me to take care of the little boy. They expected to be gone only a few minutes, as it was not far to the house of the commandant, and they did not even kiss the boy good-bye. He was playing on the floor of the isba[4]—cabin—when they left.

"I sat by the stove waiting for them to return. Time passed and I was just thinking they had been gone a long time when the door flew open and in rushed a neighbor. He was a man nearly as old as myself, Excellency. His name was Michael. He lived but two doors away with his only daughter Olga. His wife was dead many years. I scarcely knew him as he rushed in. He was wild, his clothes were torn, and blood ran down his face from a cut over his eye.

"'Gregory! Gregory!' he screamed, 'they have taken my little daughter, my pretty one, my Olechka!'

"Froth drooled from his mouth and ran down his beard, his eyes blazed, and he beat his breast with his clenched fists.

"'Man! Man!' I said, rising from my chair, 'be quiet and tell me what has happened!'

---

[4] *Izba*: peasant hut.

"He sat down on a bench and buried his face in his hands, rocking to and fro.

"'The Russians are coming and the Austrians are leaving the village. They are taking with them all the young people and are leaving the old, such as you and I, who would be only a burden to them. They came to my house and asked for my Olga'—she was a pretty girl, Excellency, not quite seventeen—'I asked them what they wanted of her, but they did not answer and tried to push by me at the door, but I barred the way. There were four soldiers and an officer in the party. The officer struck me with his riding crop, felling me to the floor. I tried to rise but a soldier jumped on me and held me down. The others rushed into place and seized my daughter and dragged her shrieking from the house. Then they tied my hands and feet and left me lying there. I worked my hands free and, unloosing my fetters, ran here, thinking you would know where they took my daughter. Hark, what is that?'

"Then, Excellency, I heard a terrible sound—the shrieks of women and the wailing of little children. 'Come!' I cried to Michael, and we ran from the house, picking up my grandson as we rushed to the street.

"I knew now why they had sent for my daughter and her husband, and I ran down the village street toward the house where they had asked her to come.

"A terrible sight met my eyes. Austrian soldiers were going about setting fire to the houses, many of which were already burning fiercely. Along the roadside, in front of her house, lay the body of old Marsha, who lived only four doors from me. Blood flowed from her chest. I stopped, but she did not move or breathe so I ran on. I ran very fast, Excellency—even carrying this child, I outdistanced Michael, who has always had something wrong with his heart.

"At the end of the village street, several companies of Austrians were drawn up in a hollow square, with the bayonets fixed on their guns. Inside the square were all the young people of the village. Barring my way was a line of soldiers drawn up across the road. They also had their bayonets fixed. The girls and young women were weeping. In front of the line of soldiers were several of the old people of the village. Some were down on their knees, begging that their dear ones be allowed to remain. One of the old men tried to force his way through the lines, but he was flung back by the Austrians.

"I rushed up to an officer who was standing there and asked to be allowed to go with my daughter. He turned on his heel and walked away. Then I heard a loud shriek and saw my daughter throw herself on one of the soldiers and try to break through the line of guards. The soldier struck her full in the face, knocking her down, and threatened her with his bayonet as she lay in the dust of the road. I saw my son-in-law. His hat was gone. His head was bowed and his hands were tied behind his back. His clothing was torn. He, too, had evidently struggled with the Austrians.

"An order was shouted and they started off down the road. One of the soldiers picked my daughter up from the ground, half dragging her along as they went.

"Then Michael, whom I had outdistanced, ran up. His face was purple and his breath coming in gasps. He saw his daughter weeping inside that square of soldiers. With a wild cry he picked up a club which was lying on the ground and dashed at the line of soldiers who barred his way. Straight at one of the soldiers he went and struck a savage blow with the club. The Austrian was a huge fellow and easily parried the blow with his rifle.

"Then I saw the soldier give a quick lunge and Michael threw up his hands, dropping the club and clutching his breast. I saw several inches of steel bayonet sticking out from between his shoulder-blades and a red streak of blood staining his white *rooboshka* (shirt). He fell to the ground, carrying the rifle with him. It stuck upright from his body. The Austrian put his big hob-nailed boot upon Michael's chest, gave a heave, and jerked the bayonet out. Michael rolled over several times and coughed, spitting out mouthfuls of blood. Finally he lay quiet.

"By this time the young folks and their guards were far off down the road. I, a feeble old man, could do nothing.

"Austrian troops came pouring through the village, which was now burning fiercely. The roads were choked with columns of artillery and ambulances, all retreating as fast as possible, their drivers yelling and swearing. Automobiles carrying officers dashed madly back and forth. Panic was in the air.

"All the time I tightly held my little grandson in my arms. He was wild with fright, screaming and crying and trying to escape from my grasp to follow his mother down the road.

"Finally I could no longer see our people. They were hidden by clouds of dust, which rose from the road. Only a few of the old folks remained. They stood stupidly about, not knowing what to do next.

"I walked back toward my house, but it was in flames. The heat was terrific and I circled the village by way of the fields. I could hear the sound of rifles and machine-guns. Some wounded Austrian soldiers came staggering down the road, making for the rear as fast as they could go.

"The fighting was getting closer and closer. Russian shells started to whistle and burst over the road, and I made off across the fields for the forest. I found a large tree which had fallen down, the limbs holding the trunk slightly off the ground. There was just room enough to hide a man's body. It was just growing dusk, so I sat down in the bushes beside the log.

"Some Austrian soldiers came running through the woods, rifles and machine-guns crashed all about, and the noise was terrible. I crawled under the log and hid, covering the little child with my body, while bullets whistled and cracked over my head and more Austrians ran by, firing their rifles as they went.

"Presently I heard Russian words spoken near me, but the firing continued as I lay still.

"I saw several soldiers creeping forward cautiously—they were Russian soldiers. The firing gradually got farther away, and when more of our soldiers came up I crawled out from under the log and called to them. They came over and talked with me, and an officer who was with them detailed a soldier to carry the child, for I was exhausted from the exertion and the excitement.

"He led the way through the forest to this very road, which was full of Russian artillery moving up in the direction of our village, and stretcher-bearers carrying the wounded back.

"We went down the road almost to where we are now seated and came to a dressing station. The doctor in charge was very kind and gave us some food and a place to sleep in his tent, but the next morning he received orders to move up closer to the fighting line, and as he could not take us with him, we had to remain here.

"Since then, we have lived in these old Austrian trenches, sleeping at night in that bomb-proof. Sometimes soldiers go by on the road and they always give us food. What we will do when the winter comes on I do not know. Occasionally I go back to where the village stood. Nothing remains there but ruins, but I go because I think possibly my daughter or her husband may escape and get back to the village looking for us, but nobody is ever there. Sometimes I meet some of my old neighbors who are living in the forest beyond the village. Do you think my daughter will escape from the Austrians, Excellency?"

The old man sat holding the sleeping child, supporting it with his arm, while his claw-like fingers stroked its golden hair.

"Can't we send him back to Rovno with a note to the Red Cross[5] asking them to look out for him?" I inquired of the Colonel.

"Yes, I think that is the best thing to do," he replied.

Our column had stopped, the horses were being fed and watered and the orderlies were having their dinner. The Colonel had our much battered victoria brought up and food was placed under the seat for the old man, the child and the driver. We gave him enough money to last him for several months and a note to the head of the Red Cross in Rovno.

At first he did not wish to go, hoping that his daughter might escape and return to the village, but we assured him that this was impossible and promised to leave word with any villagers that we might meet where he could be found, and they drove off.

"I am surprised at such atrocities from the Austrians," said the Colonel, as we rode off. "They have always been more humane than the Germans. However, they

---

[5] The Red Cross, along with other civil society organizations, took responsibility for feeding, sheltering, and caring for the millions of civilian refugees created by the war. The Great War saw the establishment of refugee services. For the refugee situation in the war, see Peter Gatrell, *A Whole Empire Walking: Refugees in Russia during World War I* (Bloomington: Indiana University Press, 1999).

receive their orders from the German General Staff and are completely under the domination of Berlin—so we may expect anything from them."

"What do you think will become of the girls those Austrians carried off?" I asked, referring to the mother of the little boy and Michael's daughter.

"What happened to the women who were seized by the Huns in the old days when they fought with clubs and spears?" the Colonel rejoined.

"You think, then, the very worst that can happen to a woman?" I queried, horrified by the thought.[6]

"Without any question!" said the Colonel; and we rode on in silence, each busy with his own thoughts.

An hour later we came to the little village in which the old peasant Gregory and his daughter and little grandson had lived, happy and content with their little existence. It was now only a charred mass of ruins, scarcely one log resting upon another.

Beyond the village we passed fields of rye and wheat, the over-ripe grain falling to the ground from the dry heads. A cloud of sparrows and wild pigeons rose from its yellow surface as we rode by. They were the only harvesters for that crop.

Near the fields we met several old men and women seated along the roadside who asked us for food. They were dirty and unkempt, in all variety of ragged garments, and were the most pitiful objects one could imagine.

We questioned them and they informed us they were from the same village as Gregory. We told them where he and the little boy could be found. They, too, were living in the forest on what they could pick up—more like wild animals than human beings. We left them sufficient food for several days and continued on our journey.

For two days we rode through a belt of devastated territory, with the sound of drum-fire in our ears day and night coming from far off in the west where lay the River Stockhod.

The terrible marks of the gigantic war machine which had rolled over the beautiful countryside were indelibly impressed on everything. In one of the swamps the Colonel and I discovered an entire battery of six-inch howitzers, a number of caissons, and a great quantity of shells for the guns. Nobody else had found them—they were so carefully screened in the heart of the swamp. They had been brought there over corduroy roads to a high spot where the ground was dry and there they had been placed. The Austrians had been too hard-pressed to get them out, and apparently had neglected to blow up the shells or even to destroy the breech blocks of the guns. There they were, their squat gray muzzles pointed toward the northeast—toward the Russian trenches abandoned a month ago.

---

[6] Grow is referring to rape, which was used by both sides as a weapon of war against civilians. For many, according to early twentieth century standards of female honor, being sexually violated was a "fate worse than death." Stories of enemy soldiers raping Russian women were very common. Russian soldiers also perpetrated such offenses, again, not only against "enemy" populations, but also against members of non-Russian nationalities within the empire.

It seemed scarcely credible that they should have remained there so long without discovery, and yet we only stumbled upon them while exploring the roads and having become lost from our columns. We took a short-cut to catch up and happened to cross this swamp, using the road which nobody had traversed since the day the Austrians had fled.

All along the roadside were isolated wooden crosses, marking the fresh graves of both Austrian and Russian dead. Where large engagements had been fought, there were great cemeteries with hundreds of these crosses, the Russians placing their dead in the cemeteries which the Austrians had established before being driven out.

I saw by my field map that we should be near the town of Kolky, on the River Styr. Its name was printed in large letters and I knew that it must be a place of importance. The country was flat, the road stretched ahead as straight as a string, and I looked for the onion-shaped church-steeple and the straw-thatched houses which mark every town in Russia and which we ought to have been able to see plainly, as we were but two miles away, according to the map. Not a sign of them could we see.

We rode forward a couple of miles and then, alongside the road, I saw acres and acres of tumbled stone and brick and burned timbers scattered about over the ground, as though some giant hand had flung them there.

"That's Kolky!" declared the Colonel.

"Kolky!" I repeated in astonishment. "Why, I thought Kolky was quite a town!"

"It was. It had a population of seven thousand. But it changed hands ten times and this is all that's left!"

All traces of any system of streets was entirely effaced, the road we followed having been cleared by the troops which preceded us through the heaps of piled-up rubbish. Not a sign of a human being was visible.

It was growing dark and we halted our horses in the midst of this scene of desolation. Several cadaverous-looking cats prowled around a heaped up pile of masonry beside the roadside. A black dog, his ribs showing on his gaunt side, came up and sniffed at us with a hungry air. He, too, looked forlorn and desolate as he circled about trying to determine if we were friend or foe. I tossed him the remains of a lunch which I had in my saddle-bag and he devoured it ravenously.

A strong raw wind had sprung up, bringing with it a cold drizzle, and I wrapped my rubber poncho tightly around me, for the rain and wind chilled me to the bone.

We spurred up our horses and rode ahead to find a place to spend the night. If we could find a place dry enough for ourselves and our orderlies to spend the night we would save the time and trouble required to put up a tent in the darkness. At the other end of the town, screened by some shell-torn trees, we found a couple of stone houses, badly battered but still retaining enough of their walls and roofs to accommodate our party. We sent word back to the column to move up, and when they arrived the horses were unhitched and tied to the ambulances and given their supper.

We spent a miserable night in the dilapidated house. Sometime in the night I was awakened by cold water soaking through my blankets, and I felt some heavy weight on my legs, as though someone were sitting on them. I reached for my flashlight and flashed it in the direction of the weight, disclosing the wretched dog that I had fed that afternoon. He was soaking wet and looked even more pathetic than before. I made him a bed in the corner and he curled himself up with the utmost satisfaction.

The next morning we crossed the River Styr on a bridge which the Russians had hastily constructed in their pursuit of the Austrians and which replaced the one which the retreating Austrians had destroyed. The dog followed at the heels of my horse, having apparently adopted me as his master, and he remained with me for several weeks, when he disappeared—being probably appropriated by some soldiers as a regiment mascot.

After crossing the river, we travelled the entire day over a military road built by the Austrians straight through the heart of an enormous swamp. The Colonel said they had used Russian prisoners to construct this marvelous piece of work.[7] Huge pilings had been driven into the marshy ground, projecting about eight feet above the surface of the mud. On these pilings rested the bed of the road made of hand hewn square timber. It was sixty feet wide, as level as a floor, and ran straight as an arrow for forty miles! The Austrians had attempted to burn it in various places as they hastily retreated, but the timber was green and not very inflammable and little damage had been done. At other points large sections had been blown up by explosives, but these had been repaired by the pursuing Russians.

The efficiency of the Austrians revealed by this gigantic piece of work served to increase our respect for the enemy we were shortly to meet, and the sound of the big guns thundering along the line of the Stockhod River far off in the west told us that the conflict was raging fiercely.

---

[7] On prisoners of war, see Alon Rachamimow, *POWs and the Great War: Captivity on the Eastern Front* (New York: Berg Publishers, 2002), and Peter Gatrell, "Prisoners of War on the Eastern Front during World War I," *Kritika: Explorations in Russian and Eurasian History* 6, no. 3 (Summer 2005): 557–66.

Chapter XX
THE BATTLE OF THE STOCKHOD

As we approached the Stockhod, the sound of the cannonade grew louder and we began to meet regiments of Siberians hurriedly marching toward the fighting line. We received word to speed up our troops, as we were needed to relieve a division which had suffered heavy losses.

We according left the heavy luggage transport wagons in a forest about five miles back of the positions and pushed on with all speed, taking only the ambulances and a wagon carrying surgical material.

When we reached the high ground three miles back from the river we could plainly trace out the fighting line for many miles north and south by the great German observation balloons hanging suspended in the air back of their lines. From one hill I counted eight of them. The Russians called them "sausages." Shrapnel could be seen bursting over the trench lines as far as the eye could see up and down the river. Our road was fortunately well screened by forest and we were able to bring our ambulances up to within half a mile of the trenches.

We established our main dressing station in the woods alongside the road which ran down to the trenches. From this point on, the road was exposed to observation, as only stunted trees grew along the sides.

The dressing station was hastily constructed from a piece of canvas stretched over a framework of poles. Sods were piled up around the four sides as a protection against H E shells and rifle bullets. There was no time to construct a dug-out. The entire thing we covered with boughs to hide it from aeroplanes, and we placed the Red Cross flag carefully beneath a small pine-tree where it was visible only to the wounded soldiers as they passed by on the road.[1]

As it grew dark I took some orderlies and two students into the trenches and established an advance dressing station in a support-trench about one hundred yards back of the fire-trench in a large dug-out which we found there.

The first-line trenches were in marshy ground and were very shallow affairs. They afforded little protection from the heavy shell fire that the Austro-Germans were pouring in on them. Our Siberians had just taken them over in the afternoon.

---

[1] Although a violation of the Geneva Convention, bombings of medical facilities were not uncommon during this war.

Looking out over No Man's Land, I wondered how it would be possible to make a successful attack. It was a great quaking marsh grown up with reeds and cattails. The Stockhod River flowed through it, dividing at this point into three branches, each about thirty yards wide. The German trenches were about four hundred yards away on top of some sand-hills which sloped up from the marsh. Down the sides of these hills could be seen the gray haze of belts of barbed wire. There were two of these hedges, each about forty feet deep, with a bare strip thirty feet wide separating them.

A road ran across the swamp, crossing the three branches of the river by small wooden bridges, now destroyed by the Austro-Germans as they retreated. This road had been built up with dirt about two feet above the surface of the swamp. Nothing could pass over it now, for it was under the direct fire from their machine-guns and artillery and was blocked at the further end by great barriers of barbed wire.

Our artillery, from the cover of the forest in the rear, was pounding the German barbed wire and first-line trenches in preparation for an attack by the infantry. The Germans were retaliating with a brisk cannonade on our first-line and communication-trenches and on the roads leading up to them. We were beginning to have a few casualties from this heavy fire, so that there was work for us as soon as we got our dressing station set up.

I found my friend Muhanoff with his company in the fire-line. He had just received his captaincy a few days before.

"You are a kind, dear friend," he declared when I congratulated him on his promotion; "but, do you know, I feel sure that I shall be a captain for only a few days. For some weeks I have had a premonition of impending death and I feel positive that it will come in the next few days."

I tried to reassure him, but I don't think I made much impression.

"This is going to be a difficult place to get across," he continued. "Just look at that marsh. When you walk out on it, they say, it quakes like so much gelatin and you sink in above your knees at each step.

"The Germans have certainly selected a beautiful line of defense. They command every inch of it from their position on the sand-hills.

"Did you hear about the artillery observers who went out on the marsh between the lines?" he asked.

"No," I replied, "what's the story?"

"Well, it shows what kind of ground we'll have to go over when we attack—which, judging from the sound of our artillery, will be sometime tomorrow morning, about the time when it becomes gray. It happened this morning. Just at dawn an officer observer and four telephone men crawled out on the marsh to establish an advanced observation point between the first two branches of the river. The telephone men carried with them the reel holding the wire, which they unwound as they advanced, letting it lay on the ground in back of them as is the usual method. They crawled out under a cover of grass and reeds and reached the spot where they were to locate the observation point. They hooked up their telephone and as it became light called up the battery saying that everything was prepared to spot the shell-breaks and correct the range when the battery began to fire. They were lying close together, concealed in the reeds. The battery fired several shots but no word came back from the observer and his crew. The battery commander called repeatedly to his observer, but the line was dead. He concluded that German shell had hit the wire and broken it, as sometimes occurs, or that the connections had become separated in some other way. He sent a lineman out from the battery to follow the wire, find the break and mend it. The man found everything intact through the forest where the wire was strung on the branches of trees and he continued on to the trench lines and then crawled out on to the marsh and through the reeds, and still he could find no break. He kept on, however, going carefully over the quaking bog on his hands and knees. Finally he came to the first branch of the river. The wire stretched out before him, clearing the river by being stretched from the reed which held it up. He got into the stream, sheltered from the sight of the Germans by the banks, and waded across. The wire ran straight to the center of a tangled growth of vegetation on that little island. The soft mud and rotting stuff shook beneath his weight so that he was fearful of sinking through. He crawled carefully on and was astonished to find the wire running right down into the mud in the center of a funnel-shaped depression. He pulled on the wire and felt something heavy on the end. He carefully hauled it up, hand over hand, getting in six or eight feet, and then through the oozy mud appeared the receiver and transmitter which, as you know, in the field telephone is in one piece. Not a sign could he find of the officer or the four men except the cap of one lying on the edge of the funnel-shaped depression. He cleaned the receiver of mud and water and called up the battery and reported the obvious solution of the mystery. The group of five men had been too heavy for the surface of the bog to hold. The tangled weeds with their roots form a sort of surface covering the liquid mass beneath, but there is a limit to its capacity, and down the five men had gone into that sticking, bottomless ooze, where they were drowned or suffocated in a few moments—and that, my boy, is the terrain over which we must attack tomorrow morning."

"Look at those crows out there on the marsh!" I exclaimed, pointing to a flock of the great black birds as they rose heavily out of the reeds and circled about over the surface of the swamp; finally settling down again in the same spot in which they had risen.

"Something dead out there," commented the Captain. "That's why they stay despite the sound of the artillery. They don't seem to mind the noise as long as there is something to eat. Imagine having them pick at your dead carcass! Ugh!" and he shuddered as he contemplated the disgusting scene.

Sometime later I recalled his horror at these vile birds, and the recollection steeled me to do something which I scarcely believe I should otherwise have attempted.

"I must be getting back to the dressing station and see that everything is in order," I said, rising from the fire-step where I had been sitting. "Come and see me to-morrow and tell me how the attack came off."

He promised to come but, as we shook hands, he added: "If I get back from the attack."

I reached the main dressing station on the edge of the woods without any adventure, although the Germans were pounding our positions pretty severely. A few wounded were coming in. They had been wounded by the shells. There was enough work to keep me up all night. Our artillery was going full blast and the Germans dropped a few shells unpleasantly near us during the night but we had no casualties in our personnel.

Just as dawn was beginning to break I heard the tell-tale sound of machine-guns and rifles, and going out onto the road could see the rockets shooting up which heralded the attack as the Captain had predicted.

A village back of the German lines was burning, set on fire by our shells, casting a lurid red glare on the clouded sky.

In a short time the lighter form of wounds—hand and arm cases—came pouring down the road, making for the dressing station, and we were all soon hard at work. After about half an hour the rifle and machine-gun fire slackened and we knew the attack was over.

The attack was unsuccessful. The German barbed wire had not been blown up sufficiently to make large gaps for our troops to get through and the Germans had an enormous number of machine-guns on the sand-hills which had not been put out of action. After suffering heavy losses on the marshy ground, our attack had broken down after almost reaching the German first-line, and what soldiers were left were forced to come back. All the wounded were soaking wet from fording the river, and all complained of the difficulty of advancing rapidly through the mud.

One fellow, a fine strapping lad of about twenty six, wounded by a bullet through the shoulder, wept bitterly while I was dressing his wound. I thought it was from the pain and told him that it would stop hurting in a few minutes.

"It is not the pain of the wound, Excellency," he sobbed. "I'm used to that. This is the third time I've been wounded. But now I've got to go to the base hospital for heaven knows how long, and so far I have never even seen a German, much less get my bayonet into one!"

The Russian soldier can stand more pain without a murmur that I had believed it possible for the human organism to bear. They were the most patient, enduring fellows, and as fine soldiers as I think the world has ever seen. I speak of the old days—when we had good morale and discipline in the Russian army. These men simply could not be downed. They would sit in the trenches and be blown to pieces—regiment after regiment—when they did not have shells to reply to the Germans and when they could see nothing to shoot at.

There is no greater test of the bravery of troops than holding fast to a position when they are smothered in artillery fire from long range guns and have nothing with which to hit back at the enemy. Yet these Russians did it time and time again in the early days of the war—when the very trenches in which they sat were entirely obliterated by shell fire and whole regiments were annihilated without firing a single shot.[2]

But to get back to our story. I worked on through the morning until nearly midday, and was wondering what had befallen my friend Captain Muhanoff when a soldier approached the dressing station and addressing me said: "I am a soldier in Captain Muhanoff's company. He was killed this morning in an attack and Lieutenant Saparoff of his company sent me to tell you."

"Muhanoff dead!" I exclaimed, stunned by the news. "No, it cannot be!"

"Yes, Excellency, it is so. We're all heartbroken. We loved him. He was like a father to us. After the attack this morning all that was left of our company, which had numbered two hundred, was sixty. I saw the Captain fall. We had lost heavily going across that awful marsh.

"He was ahead of us as always in an attack. We followed, dropping by the dozens from the terrible machine-gun fire. We couldn't go faster than a walk, for at each step we sank in above the knees in mud and water. It was just getting daylight and the Captain had reached the first line of German barbed wire. He was going along the edge, stooping low and looking for an opening. He went only a few steps when he seemed to find a place where he could get through, for he turned and beckoned for us to come on, and then started through the opening. I saw him throw up his hands and fall backward and to the side into the barbed wire. His coat caught in some wire which had not been broken and his body fell backward, bending over the wire, the arms hanging down. He was quite dead when I rushed up. I was about to try to get him down and carry him back when I heard the whistle of the Lieutenant, who was now in command, sound the retreat. The few who were left of our company turned and went back through the marsh as fast as they could go, and I knew it was certain death to remain, so I came back, leaving the Captain hanging on the wire. When I got back to the trenches I looked back over the marsh and I could see him still hanging there, held up by the wire. He can be seen quite plainly, and if you will come to the trenches with me I will show him to you."

We had about completed our work and no more wounded were coming in, so I accompanied the soldier to the first-line trench. He put his rifle through a loophole, sighting it carefully across the marsh toward the German lines.

"Look now, Excellency," he said; "the front sight is pointing directly to the body of the Captain if you line it up with the rear sight."

---

[2] As indicated in the introduction, this was an overly optimistic view that did not account for the numerous problems the Russian army faced prior to 1917, including fraternization, desertion, insubordination, and other forms of lack of discipline.

I could plainly see a gray-brown object hanging from the front of the first wire hedge, and through my binoculars I studied carefully the ground surrounding the body, fixing in my mind its relation to various landmarks. There was something terrible for me in the fact that my friend's body hung out there on that wire and would continue to hang there until it became a horrid putrefying object on the landscape unless something were done. As I stood occupied with these distressing thoughts, the soldier at my side kept staring out through the loophole at the body of his late captain, fascinated, I suppose, by the horror of the thing. All of a sudden he fired, and before I could say a word he let go four more shots in rapid succession.

"My God, man!" I exclaimed. "Stop! Have you gone mad?"

He was firing point-blank at the Captain's body!

"The crows, Excellency, the crows!" he exclaimed, continuing to fire as fast as he could work the bolt action of his rifle.

A sickening sight met my eyes as I looked through my binoculars. There were two crows in the air, hovering around the head of the Captain's corpse, and a third sat on his shoulder. Its head was moving with short vicious stabs in a most significant manner.

The soldier beside me was cramming a fresh clip of cartridges into his rifle and I could hear him sobbing as he worked. On my left stood another soldier, gazing stolidly out over No Man's Land through the next loophole. He was paying no attention to us but watching for a glimpse of a German or an Austrian in the trenches beyond. I snatched his rifle from his hands and before he realized what had happened was rapidly firing out of my loophole, aiming directly for a black spot against the brown background. The soldier at my right was also firing slowly and deliberately. Thank God! That hideous black bird suddenly took wing—startled by the impact of a bullet on the barbed wire or some nearby object, and sailed off. We both stopped firing and heaved a sigh of relief, and I handed the empty rifle back to the astonished soldier.

"Will you stand watch here until tonight and shoot at them if they come back, providing I get the permission of your company commander?" I asked the soldier.

"Yes, surely," he eagerly replied.

"Tonight I shall cross that marsh and bring his body back if it is the last thing I ever do!"

"And I shall accompany you, Excellency. Without my help you could never find the body, much less carry it back."

"Very well; you remain here and I'll join you at nine o'clock this evening when it is beginning to grow dark. It will be clear and I think we'll be able to locate it by that big pine-tree and the bushes on this side."

I obtained the necessary permission for the soldier to remain on watch and also told the commander of the regiment which held the line at that point of my plan to rescue the Captain's corpse. He consented but warned me of the danger of the undertaking.

"Be sure and get back before twelve because we will probably attack again at that time," he added. Metia, the student, hearing of my plans, requested permission to accompany me. He was always on the lookout for some adventure and this affair was to his liking, and I consented.

At nine o'clock we joined the soldier.

"The crows did not return again," he reported, "but if we don't get him in tonight, they are sure to be back tomorrow."

Snipers on both sides were firing occasional shots, and every now and again a machine-gun would let go with a sputter. Our artillery was hammering away in a methodical manner, and the Germans were replying with a moderate fire on our first lines.

While it was still dusk we slid over the parapet cautiously into the long grass in front of the trenches and crawled out through a gap in our wire, which was only a few rows in thickness. We wormed our way carefully through the grass out onto the marsh, where we were protected by the tall reeds and could advance with less caution although still forced to crawl on our hands and knees. Metia and I carried revolvers and the soldier had his rifle. The pine-tree standing out against the after-glow from the sun looked black as ink and we had no trouble in keeping a direct course. We forded two branches of the river and crawled out on the boggy ground that separated them from the third branch. It was very soft, so that we sunk in almost to our elbows when our weight rested on our hands. We were soaking wet but did not feel cold.

We could not advance farther until it was quite dark, and lay quietly in the reeds waiting. Occasionally a bullet would hit with a *plop* in the marsh near us, and the Germans began to throw rockets up occasionally as it grew dark.

When it was quite dark, we started forward again. We had to be on the watch for German patrols and wiring parties which were certain to be out on No Man's Land, the latter to repair the damage done their barbed wire by our artillery during the day. After we had waded through the third branch of the river, which came up almost to our armpits, and were advancing across the next piece of marsh, I heard a regular dull pounding and knew that this was a German wiring party driving stakes with a wooden mallet wrapped in cloths to muffle the sound. They seemed to be several hundred feet away and as they would probably be intent on their work I did not fear detection and crept cautiously forward. When I reached the bushes which I had spotted during the afternoon, I could see the stakes of the German entanglements, and directly in front of me and not forty feet away was a dark object hanging from the first strands of the barricade. The pounding continued on the right and occasionally I could hear the guttural sound of voices speaking German, but I could not distinguish any members of the party.

Just as we reached the wire, not ten feet from the body, a rocket rose from the German trenches about seventy yards away. I felt as though I must have stood out before their view as plain as an actor on the stage with a big calcium spotlight on him. We lay perfectly flat on the grass until it died down, and as nothing happened we decided we had not been seen.

I felt as though a million eyes were peering down the slope of the hill at us as we crawled up to the body and carefully and noiselessly disengaged it from the wires on which it was caught. Barbed wire is like the strings of a piano when stretched and the slightest thing catching in it or striking it produces a loud tang audible for some distance, so we had to be extremely careful.

We got it down, however, and started crawling slowly back, Metia and I taking hold of the Captain's icy hands and dragging him between us while the soldier brought up the rear watching and listening carefully for danger.

We had reached the clump of bushes about forty feet from the wire when I heard the soldier hiss sharply through his teeth. We stopped crawling and lay perfectly flat. We could hear the swish of the marsh grass as several persons approached. I reached for my revolver and Metia did the same. We thought we were surely in for it as the sound of tramping men approached. Three dark forms appeared in the gloom between us and the wire, walking slowly along, examining the entanglements. If they had seen the body before they evidently did not notice its absence, for they passed on toward the left.

It was a difficult job getting our pathetic burden through the streams and the thick weeds of the bog beyond, but we eventually reached our barbed wire without mishap, and when we reached the trench parapet waiting hands received the body as we slid it down, dripping wet from its passage through the river and marsh.

I was soaked to the skin and the night air was cool, but great beads of perspiration were running down my face as a result of my exertions. I thanked the soldier who had accompanied us.

"*Nichevo*, Excellency," he replied. "I could not do less for our poor Captain."

The next day we gently lowered the body of the brave fellow into his last resting-place and placed over his grave a rough wooden cross on which was burned, with a hot iron, his name, regiment and the date of his death.

I felt glad that we had been able to give him a decent burial. I know that had we not recovered his body I would have been haunted all my life by the vision of that dangling form on the barbed wire with the carrion crows hovering around it for their horrid work.

The horrible conditions which exist in No Man's Land after heavy fighting is one of the things that makes the war so awful to the man in the trenches.

Chapter XXI
WE BREAK THROUGH!

All day our artillery had kept up an intense fire on the German lines. Fresh regiments from our corps replaced the ones depleted by the previous attack.

Engineer battalions worked all day in the forest, felling trees and cutting the logs into pieces suitable for bridge building. Should the attack prove successful, it would be necessary to rebuild the three bridges that led across the marsh.

These timbers were carried to the edge of the forest by the road, under the protection of the screening trees, and were placed in regular order so that no confusion would result if it became necessary to put them in place at night when all of the work would have to be done in darkness, for the enemy commanded the road from their position on the sand-hills.

At ten o'clock our Siberians made a terrific attack, wave after wave of men being sent over the marsh in the face of a devastating fire from German machine-guns, rifles and artillery.

Despite their enormous losses they stormed the Austro-German positions, carrying all three lines of defense and driving them back to the depth of five meters beyond the river.

Attacks were carried out all along the lines for the distance of twenty kilometers, but our corps was the only one to penetrate the German positions. The result was that both flanks failed to advance and an extremely difficult problem developed.

Our men were across the river and consolidating their lines four miles back from the stream in the center. From this point our position sloped back in a curving line toward either flank where the supporting troops had failed to cross the river. In other words, we had penetrated on a six-mile front to a depth of four miles at the deepest point, forming a nasty salient open to a flanking fire from the Austro-German guns.

Running through the center of this salient was the single road through which all supplies to the advanced lines had to be carried. The wounded also had to be brought over this road. As it was raised above the level of the flat marsh, standing out in plain view of the enemy observers, anything attempting to cross was under their direct fire. The engineer battalion rushed up bridge parts, and by the time the first streaks of dawn appeared in the east, we received word the bridges were completed.

The commander of the fourth regiment, which was holding the extreme end of the salient across the river, called up by telephone asking us to move our dressing station up as nearly as possible to the newly established first-line and to bring some ambulances over as soon as possible, for there were hundreds of wounded lying about in the fields.

I accordingly ordered five ambulances and a wagon carrying supplies to be in readiness to start across the road for the other side, and Metia and I rode ahead to pick out the location for this advanced dressing station.

As we came to the edge of the forest and looked out over the road we saw that it was a spouting lane of flying dirt and smoke from the German shells where they were trying to destroy the newly constructed bridges and to wreck the surface of the road with shell holes. I could see a number of dead horses stretched out on the roadside.

They were from a mountain battery which had crossed just at daybreak. Not a living thing was visible—indeed, nothing could possibly live in that welter of flying shell fragments.

We stopped our horses and surveyed the lane of death over which we had to pass to reach the other side.

"Do you think we can make it, Metia?" I asked.

His face was dead white and his jaw set. "We have to make it!" he answered grimly.

We could perhaps have walked it in greater safety, but the commander had ordered us to hurry and I decided to take it at a gallop and take a chance. The five ambulances and the supply wagon drove up and I ordered them to wait until we reached the other side.

"When I wave my handkerchief from the edge of the woods on the sand-hills," I commanded, "whip up your horses and come over at a gallop. Scatter out well and, if anyone is hit, stop and pick him up and bring him with you but let the horse and ambulance remain."

"*Tak tochena!* (Yes, surely)" they replied in chorus; and that was always the way when told to do anything—no matter how impossible the task might seem.

We gave our ponies the spurs and started across. We bent low in the saddle, and the torn surface of the road seemed simply to fly by as our ponies, excited by the scream of the shell and the crashing explosions, lengthened their stride.

We were a quarter of the way across when my pony suddenly braced his feet under him, slid a few yards and came to a dead stop, almost throwing me over his head, so sudden was the movement. Metia reined in his horse, narrowly missing running me down. My pony was now rearing, his front feet pawing the air. He tried to turn back but I plied the spurs and whipped him cruelly with my Cossack knout.

I saw now what the trouble was. Lying on the side of the road was a dead artillery horse, his feet sticking out in the road, and my pony was afraid to pass him. He snorted and shied as the shells burst unpleasantly near him with loud reports and the air hummed with deadly flying fragments. I shouted to Metia to ride on, thinking that if my horse saw the other one go by the dead animal he would follow. Metia dashed ahead, and after spurring and beating him my pony followed.

We thundered over the first bridge. The second bridge had been hit by a shell and some engineers who had been lying under cover of the embankment were busy repairing it. We crossed the third bridge and finally galloped into the protecting grove of trees, and I rode back to the edge of the wood to a high ridge where I could be seen by our drivers on the other side and waved a handkerchief in the air. As I had half suspected, the thing had really looked worse from the other end of the road than it really was, for the shells were not so close together as they appeared to be.

After a few minutes I saw the ambulances shoot out of the forest and start across the road, the horses galloping and the dust flying.

Everything went well until they were half-way across. Then apparently they were seen by the Austro-German observers, for I saw the yellow white puff of shrapnel directly above them. The second ambulance veered to the side of the road, the horse stumbling and falling, and the ambulance overturned. The driver was thrown out in the middle of the road and lay, a little inert spot, on the brown surface of the road. The ambulance immediately in back of him stopped and I saw the driver leap out, gather his fallen companion in his arms, place him in the ambulance, leap back on the driver's seat and whip up his horse.

The Germans continued to rain shrapnel down on them, but were timing their shells badly, so that they burst beyond the road and the remainder of the party reached the sheltering growth of trees in safety. I found that the driver had been struck in the shoulder by a shrapnel ball which passed through downward and forward, emerging from his chest just below the collar-bone. We hastily bound him up, put him in the ambulance, and went on. The road was fairly well screened by trees and we were able to reach our troops, who were occupying the captured third line of Austrian trenches.

Leaving the ambulances under some trees, I started for these trenches just as our soldiers left them in another attack against the Austro-Germans, who were desperately endeavoring to defend a small village which had been partly destroyed by our artillery.

They had numerous machine-gun emplacements and strong dug-outs in this village, but our troops, although they lost heavily, were able to force them out. I could see them advancing beyond the village after a few moments of sharp fighting. If they drove the Austro-Germans back far enough I saw that this village would make an ideal location for an advanced dressing station, so I cautiously followed up on foot toward the village.

Wounded Austrians, Germans and Russians lay sprawled on the ground together, and a great many dead on both sides were scattered thickly about. The village was a tumbled mass of ruins, part of which was still smoking from the recent fire caused by our artillery.

I noticed the entrance to a large dug-out along the edge of the village. Several telephone wires, which the Germans had not had time to remove, led down into it. I decided it would make an excellent dressing station, for it had thick walls and would stand heavy shelling.

Before I went down the steps I examined my revolver, as I had no hand-grenades with me and I recalled a similar experience I had had early in my trench-warfare adventures.

The dug-out was dark and as I entered I could just make out a rough table littered with papers. Then there was a sudden stabbing flash of light from the side, the sharp crack of a revolver, and I felt a stinging pain in my abdomen. With the flash, I fired, blindly aiming at the direction from which it had come, leaning partly over the table to do so, and jumped back from the door.

I felt weak and giddy, and beads of perspiration were on my forehead. I unloosened my clothing and found that the bullet which had struck me had just grazed the skin, producing a red wheal across my abdomen. In the language of the old hunters of central Pennsylvania, I had been "scutched."

I sat down on one of the steps to regain my composure. As I had leaped back through the door I had heard something metallic clatter to the floor of the dug-out and now I could hear a shuffling and the sound of labored breathing coming from inside. Then I heard a drip, drip, drip, as though water was spilling from some overturned vessel on to the floor of the dug-out. I waited possibly five minutes and then, still holding my revolver, I peered into the dark interior. As my eyes became accustomed to the gloom I saw a man in the gray uniform of Germany seated on a bench beside the table. He was leaning back, his head resting against the wall and turned to one side. As he did not move I stepped into the dug-out and, pointing my revolver at him, walked over and pushed him on the shoulder. He slid limply off the side of the bench, his body resting against its arm.

Blood was flowing from a wound in his left chest just above the heart and, running down over the bench and dropping to the floor, had produced the sound which I had heard. On the floor lay the latest type of German automatic revolver. By his uniform I saw that he was an under-officer,[1] and when I came to examine him I found that he had a slight wound from a bullet through the left arm.

I had killed him with my first shot, merely by chance, for I did not see him and only fired at the flash of his gun.

In discussing the incident later with the commander of the regiment, he told me that the German officers had told their men that the Russians were attacking with Cossacks who, when they took prisoners, always cut their tongues out and their ears off, and this under-officer, having been wounded and fearing capture, had evidently

---

[1] A non-commissioned officer (NCO).

decided to sell his life as dearly as possible when he saw me enter the dug-out, rather than be captured.

We established our advanced dressing station in the dug-out and proceeded to take care of the wounded Germans and Russians. Our lines had been advanced another mile beyond the village and here, encountering strong resistance, our men had dug themselves in.

We remained in this situation for ten days, during which the enemy made eleven desperate counter-attacks, but they were unable to break through. It was an extremely difficult task to get our wounded back over the road across the marsh. We could send them only at night, for the Germans, although they could plainly distinguish the Red Cross on the side of our ambulances, never lost an opportunity to pour a terrific fire on the wounded-laden carts.

The German system of shelling Red Cross dressing stations and ambulance columns and firing on the wounded as they crawl back to their lines is to my mind one of the significant things of this war.

Were it done by a savage, unlearned people such as the wild African, one could understand it, but when ordered by the highest officials of a so-called Kultured[2] race it points out with startling vividness the great menace which threatens the civilized world. It has a very distinct object: namely, to instill into the minds of our peasant soldier an absolute loathing and horror of the war—in other words, to break his morale.

Whether it will accomplish its purpose I cannot say, but it surely will show clearly to all thinking people that the Potsdam ring must be broken. Germany must not, shall not, win this war!

---

[2] Here Grow uses the German word *Kultur* seemingly ironically, as it used to designate what the Germans understood as a higher level of development, superior to both the West and the East.

Chapter XXII
A BLIND ARMY

The bridges were destroyed every day by the German artillery and repaired every night by our engineer battalions while our troops were attacking and the Germans could not devote much attention to the roads in the rear of our lines. It was a case of building three bridges a day and as we remained in this position for ten days our engineers practically rebuilt thirty bridges!

One night I started to ride back toward our main dressing station, but on arriving at the first bridge I found my progress arrested by a long, tightly massed column of artillery limbers, transport wagons, ambulances loaded with wounded, and field kitchens which were crossing to the other side. Their way was blocked by a damaged bridge which the engineers were repairing.

I could hear the sound of dozens of hammers, the low commands of the officers, and the splashing of hundreds of men who were working in the cold water which came up to their arm-pits. A German searchlight came creeping down the road, and as we sat there waiting impatiently for the completion of the bridge, unable to go either forward or backward because of the congestion, we realized that if the German observers spotted us they would make a nasty mess of the closely packed transport.

A shell came moaning up the marsh. The drivers heard it and sudden panic broke out as they leaped from their wagons and flattened themselves on the ground underneath. It was one of those high angle shells that you can hear for a long time as it comes, but there was nothing to do but wait until it landed. It wailed over our heads and burst in back of us in some reserve-trenches. A second shell landed near the first one, and I was certain that the Germans were firing at the trenches two hundred yards away and not at us at all. I called to the drivers and told them to get back on their wagons, and after another short wait the word was given that the bridge was ready and we all crossed safely to the other side without further incident.

Toward the end of the battle of the Stockhod it became necessary for us to dislodge several companies of German troops from some high ground in a field where they had dug themselves in shallow pits. They had erected machine-guns and commanded a considerable sweep of territory. The field was half a mile across and it was decided to use Cossack cavalry in the attack instead of infantry, as it was believed the cavalry would sustain fewer losses.

A regiment of Cossacks was accordingly brought up under the cover of the forest which faced the field. Our men had dug in along the edge of this woods but had not erected barbed wire, so that the Cossacks could pass directly over our trenches as they charged.

A shrill whistle sounded and the Cossacks burst out from under the trees with loud yells, their horses leaping our narrow trenches and galloping across the field for the German positions on the hillside.

Each man was armed with a fourteen-foot lance with a knife-like steel point, a great curved sabre at his side with a blade like that of a razor, a short dagger with a nasty two-edge blade in the belt, and a carbine on a leather strap slung across the shoulder.

They made a wonderful picture as they galloped across that field. They had scarcely covered half the distance when the German artillery put up a heavy barrage of shrapnel over them, and the machine-guns and rifles were also taking a heavy toll. Every here and there I could see a horse and rider go down and roll over in a confused tangle on the ground.

Despite their losses, however, the regiment got to the Austrian positions. After running the Austrians through with their long lances, the Cossacks would ride by and disengage their weapons by a strong pull. Occasionally, however, the lance would be torn from their grasp, and then out would flash their long keen sabers. I attended a number of Germans after this fight, which showed the deadly power of the Cossack cutting stroke. They use a free-arm swing quite different from the lunge which the American, German, English, and Swedish cavalrymen use.

One man I attended had his entire arm and shoulder carried away by a single blow from a sabre. Another poor devil had been struck in the top of the head and he was split through to his breast-bone, the skull cut as clean as though the work had been done with a saw.

I did not believe that a sabre could do such deadly work until I saw the Cossacks practicing their cutting stroke. They erected about ten birch stakes in the ground, one being placed about every ten feet. The stakes were about five feet high and four or five inches in diameter. The Cossack started his horse at a gallop, rode down on the right or left side of the line of stakes, and with every leap of the horse as he passed a stake there was a lightning move of the arm, a sound of steel cleaving the air, a sharp metallic clink, and the top of the post flew off in the shape of a neatly severed block about two inches thick—cut from the entire thickness of the post.[1]

When the Cossacks had effectually disposed of the occupants of the German trenches they sent their horses back in groups of ten, each group being urged on by a Cossack on horseback. They came flying riderless back across the field, the Austrian

---

[1] For more on the Cossacks' military training and way of life, see Shane O'Rourke, *The Cossacks* (Manchester: Manchester University Press, 2007).

shrapnel bursting above them. Many were struck but the majority reached the shelter of the forest. The Cossacks turned their light machine-guns, which they had taken with them strapped to the backs of some of the horses, upon the German trenches to the right and left and rendered them almost untenantable. In the confusion caused by this rapid move our infantry was able to advance across the field, reinforcing the Cossacks, with very few losses.

After the action was over I found that my horse was gone. He had apparently been hit by a piece of shell, had torn loose and run off, carrying with him a new camera and a greatly prized poncho which had served me well on many occasions. I afterward learned from some soldiers who had seen my horse galloping wildly along that he had run directly into the German trenches, carrying with him my two most valued possessions.

Our tired regiments were finally withdrawn when it was found impossible to advance the flanks across the river, and fresh divisions were put in their place.

We packed up our equipment and proceeded back to Rovno, where we boarded trains and started for the same positions we had vacated in late July—just south of Lake ———.[2] Here, in September, 1916, our sadly depleted corps took up a quiet sector about twenty kilometers long and waited for something to turn up.

The great drive of Brusiloff was halted only by the terrible character of the marshy ground over which our brave troops had had to attack and by the lack of artillery and shells, for near the end of the fighting we were running very short of everything.[3]

On several occasions after having taken German trenches our troops had found themselves without even rifle cartridges or grenades. We had no aeroplanes worth mentioning for observation.[4] During the entire Russian offensive I saw only one Rus-

---

[2] Again, most likely this was Lake Naroch, in northwestern Belarus.

[3] By 1916, most of the shortages that plagued the Russian Army previously had been resolved. There were sufficient stocks of machine-guns, shells, and rifles for frontline units. Moreover, during the course of the attack, the Russians were able to capture hundreds of Austrian weapons. The only real area of deficiency was in experienced officers, as most of those who had begun the war with training had been killed off as a result of the brave—but rather strategically unsound—practice of leading troops into battle.

[4] Imperial Russia actually possessed a large fleet of aircraft when the war broke out in 1914, totaling 244 aircraft, second only to Germany's 250. But many of its airplanes were outdated and difficult to coordinate, stretched out over the length of the long Eastern Front, and suffered heavy losses from the start of the war. The Russians did purchase a number of aircraft from the American Curtiss company, but the planes arrived in such poor condition that they could not be used. See Scott W. Palmer, *Dictatorship of the Air: Aviation Culture and the Fate of Modern Russia* (Cambridge: Cambridge University Press, 2006), and Timothy Wilson, "A Story Untold: The Imperial Russian Air Force, 1909–1917" (PhD diss., Pennsylvania State University, 2001).

sian aeroplane, an old type of Farnum biplane,⁵ so slow that it seemed merely to crawl across the sky on the one occasion that I saw it up. It had barely got under way when twelve German planes, all of the newest and swiftest type of fighting machines, began to close in upon it, and the Russian flier had to descend immediately.

Ours was a blind army unable to tell what the enemy was doing while they were aware of every move we made.

Despite these enormous handicaps, however, our troops, in the space of three months, captured 400,000 prisoners and took many hundreds of miles of territory from the enemy. By their bravery they released the pressure on the Italians early in the summer and preserved them from inevitable disaster.⁶

---

⁵ Similar to a Wright Model B biplane, a fixed-wing aircraft with two main wings stacked one above the other.

⁶ The offensive was also successful in forcing the Germans to end their attack against the British and French at Verdun in order to shift their forces to the Eastern Front, and in convincing the Romanians to enter the conflict as part of the Entente.

Chapter XXIII
THE GAS ATTACK

At five o'clock on the morning of the ninth of September, 1916, the wind was coming gently from the German lines toward ours with a scarcely perceptible movement. Metia and I were sleeping in our dug-out about three hundred yards back of the first-line trenches.

I was awakened by the sound of a heavy bombardment from our artillery and the screeching and sharp explosions of German shells landing near our dug-out. I aroused Metia and proceeded to get ready to go down to the trenches to find out what was up. I slipped my gas-mask over my shoulder as I threw on my clothes, although while it was a rule that officers and soldiers should always wear gas-masks when within two miles of the trenches, we were all rather careless in that respect. Indeed, we frequently found upon examining the soldiers' masks that the box containing the chemicals designed to neutralize the gas had been emptied and contained instead tobacco, bread, or similar articles! Our corps had never experienced a really severe gas attack and our carelessness was more or less natural.[1]

As Metia and I approached the trenches, I saw ahead what looked to be a swirling bank of fog rolling down on us. It was only about fifty feet high and it crept slowly and heavily, seeming to flow along the surface of the earth with a hideous writhing motion.[2]

I realized immediately what it was and shouted to Metia to put on his gas-mask, proceeding at the same time to slip my own on. If you don't get the mask on before you get a lungful of gas, it is usually fatal. I had just got my mask into place when I was surrounded by the flying wreaths of the yellow vapor and I heard an awful cry and a violent coughing and choking back of me. I turned and saw Metia on the ground, writhing like a chicken with its head off. I ran back to him and tried to lift him from

---

[1] Preparations for protection of troops against gas attacks had not been undertaken with serious dedication by the Russian military medical services, and as a result, many suffered from its effects. The troops were not properly educated on how to use gas masks, and many did not understand the lethal threat gas posed, and even mistrusted the gas masks they had issued. For more on this subject, see Steven J. Main, "Gas on the Eastern Front During the First World War (1915–1917)," *The Journal of Slavic Military Studies* 28, no. 1 (2015): 99–132.

[2] The type of gas used by the Germans was chlorine, a deadly and quick-acting form of poison.

the ground and get him back out of the gas, but it was too late! So dense was the mass of vapor that in five minutes after he took the first breath of the vile stuff, he was dead! He had come off without his mask and in the excitement and darkness I had not noticed its absence.

There was nothing to do for the poor boy and I left him and continued down to the first line. Not a single rifle shot was being fired and I wondered whether all our men had been gassed.

When I reached the trenches the upper air was growing pure, but the gas still clung to the bottom of the trenches, and in the bomb-proofs it was very dense.

The sight that met my eyes in the trenches, I shall never forget.

Dozens of men were lying about in the bottom of the trenches. Most of them were dead but a few were still choking and breathing with horrid rattling gasps. As I flashed my lantern on their contorted faces I saw that from every mouth exuded a great heaped-up pile of greenish-white froth. With the help of my orderlies we proceeded to drag these poor wretches out of the holes where they had perished like rats in a trap. As we worked, a second and third wave of gas passed over us, and following each wave the Germans attacked. Fortunately the attacks were weak and scattered and our machine-gun men, who had been able to get their masks on in time, broke them up with comparative ease.

In that small sector, the deadly fumes killed no less than two thousand of our men.[3] The stuff penetrated to a distance of some ten miles in the rear of our lines, following the low ground, like a river flowing through a valley, and at this great distance killed some cows and horses in a field.

There was not much to do for the chaps who had been slightly gassed. The two hundred whom we succeeded in getting out alive suffered intense agony at every breath, but we quieted them with morphine and sent them back in the ambulances to the division hospital.

By ten o'clock fresh regiments had replaced the one which had been wiped out, and the two thousand dead bodies were carried back to the cemetery in back of the lines, where they were placed row after row, covering half an acre of ground. Poor Metia was buried with the rest of them.

---

[3] These numbers may be an exaggeration, but it is possible that casualties were quite heavy. In a previous attack by the Germans using chlorine gas on May 31, 1915, 1,183 died from poisoning.

Chapter XXIV
THE REVOLUTION

After the gas attack we settled down to the quiet monotonous business of trench warfare.

It was noticeable that the morale of the soldiers was not what it should have been. The long, arduous campaign of more than two and a half years was beginning to tell on them.

Many of them came from villages thousands of miles away from the fighting front—indeed most of the Siberians came from the provinces on the Pacific Coast over five thousand miles away. The military authorities found it impracticable to give them leaves of absence and many of them hadn't seen their families since the start of the war.

The remoteness of their homes from the German frontier naturally led them to feel that the danger of German invasion was a far cry. Then, too, the knowledge that all was not well in Petrograd, that military secrets were given away, that there was corruption in the munitions department, and that they were fighting an uphill fight without the proper support at home had a very depressing effect on the men. The letters they received from home told them of food shortages and they were anxious to return and provide for their own. Not only was the food situation serious in the cities but we were beginning to feel it in the army too. The bread was bad and meat was scarce—in fact, there was very little fresh meat at all and disastrous epidemics of scurvy assailed our men and materially reduced our fighting forces.

An army must be fed and fed well and there is nothing that so reduces the morale of soldiers in field or barracks as bad rations. The soldiers were tired of it all.

In mid-winter the news of the death of Rasputin came to us, and with his bad influence removed everybody felt more hopeful.[1]

---

[1] Grigori Rasputin was a notorious figure at the court of Tsar Nicholas II. He was a Siberian monk belonging to an Orthodox sect known as *khlysty*, who managed to ingratiate himself with the royal family by claiming to have the ability to control the hemorrhaging of the hemophiliac tsarevich Alexei, youngest child and only son (and therefore heir to the throne) of Nicholas II. His reputation was one of drunkenness and licentiousness, and public opinion widely held that he manipulated the tsar and tsarina, even influencing policy. Most of this was pure rumor and speculation, but nonetheless, he was seen as a powerful and nefarious character. As a result, a small group of aristocratic elites, who believed him to have undue and

In November Colonel Kalpaschnecoff had gone to America to endeavor to obtain some motor ambulances, of which we were greatly in need, and on January 1st, 1917, another doctor having been found to take my place, I left the front to help him in this work.

I arrived in Petrograd on January 4th. It was twenty degrees below zero and long lines of people were standing from early morning till mid-day waiting for the opportunity to buy food from the stores—which had very little to sell.[2]

They were a patient lot, as they stood for hours shivering in their scanty garments. Several small demonstrations had been made in the squares, the poor souls clamoring for food. The price of clothing was extremely high. A pair of ordinary shoes cost $40. Wood, which was used altogether as fuel in Petrograd, was out of reach of the poor people. Rumors were going about of trouble, but no one looked for a real revolution.

I finally obtained passage on a steamer sailing for America and on reaching there found, much to my delight, that we had at last decided to come into the war.

I left Petrograd in the middle of January and arrived in Christiana about the 20th. When it was time to sail the submarine blockade had been declared by Germany and it was impossible for our boat to proceed to Kirkwall for examination, and the English would not allow it to sail without it. Consequently I had to remain in Christiana until March. While there the news of the Revolution[3] reached me and came as a great surprise.

---

pernicious influence at court, conspired to kill him. The story of his murder is as fantastical as his life—being poisoned, shot, stabbed, and, finally, drowned. For more on Rasputin, see Douglas Smith, *Rasputin: Faith, Power, and the Twilight of the Romanovs* (New York: Farrar, Straus and Giroux, 2016).

[2] Shortages of food and other necessities plagued the Russian home front throughout the war, but became increasingly acute in early 1917.

[3] Here Grow is referring to the first revolution that occurred in Russia in 1917, known as the February Revolution, as it began on February 24 according to the old Russian calendar, but on March 7, New Style. It began with protests in the streets by women demanding bread, but soon became widespread demonstrations against the war and the tsarist government. Tsarist officials were unable to restore order, and Nicholas II was convinced to renounce the throne. He had hoped his younger brother Mikhail would assume the crown, but the latter refused. Russia was proclaimed a social democracy, and in the absence of a ruler, the Russian parliament, or Duma, created a twelve-man Provisional Government to run the country until such time as a constituent assembly could be held, comprised of elected officials, who would then determine the future course of Russia. Simultaneously, councils, or soviets, of worker, peasant, and soldier representatives were created, the most important of which being the Petrograd Soviet of Soldiers' and Workers' Deputies, which essentially coexisted with the Provisional Government in a situation historians describe as "dual power." See Tsuyoshi Hasegawa, *The February Revolution, Petrograd, 1917: The End of the Tsarist Regime and the Birth of Dual Power*, rev. ed. (Leiden: Brill, 2017).

THE REVOLUTION

In July I was sent back to Russia on a mission for the Red Cross. On landing at Vladivostock[4] I was struck by the change in the appearance and conduct of the Russian soldiers.[5]

There were thousands of them wandering aimlessly about, with apparently nothing else to do but listen to the countless speeches being made at every street-corner. They were no longer clad in decent uniforms but slouched about in nondescript garments, their boots covered with mud and dust, listlessly smoking cigarettes.

They no longer saluted their officers. Their soldierly bearing was gone. The insidious preaching of German propagandists had sapped their moral fiber.

On the trip across Siberia I saw thousands of soldiers traveling back from the front, crowding the trains to suffocation-point. There was little disorder other than the speech-making which occurred at every station. Invariably there was at least one individual who advanced the idea that America was in the war only for the purpose of gain, and suggested that the best thing for the soldiers to do was to leave the front and go back to their villages, where they could seize the land from the land-holders and divide it among themselves. These orators were palpably the paid agents of Germany.[6]

In Siberia were hundreds of thousands of Austrian and German prisoners who had been living for months in the villages, tilling the land of the soldiers who were at the front, living in their homes and exerting a most harmful influence. In many cases they had assumed in all respects the functions of the head of the house in the cottages where they lived. The soldiers at the front knew this and it naturally had a bad effect upon them, for they wished to return and oust the parasites. The situation was undoubtedly brought about by people high up in court circles who were pro German

---

[4] City in Russia's Far East, on the Pacific Coast, not far from the Chinese border. Later, it would become the staging point for the Allied intervention to attempt to overthrow the Bolsheviks.

[5] Although Grow does not mention it, changes in army discipline were largely the result of Order No. 1, issued by the Petrograd Soviet in March 1917. It eliminated many forms of old discipline, including corporal punishment, required officers to address their soldiers with the formal "you" (*vy*), and granted soldiers the ability to form committees to make decisions about orders. While it was intended only for the troops of the Petrograd garrison in an attempt to stabilize its quickly deteriorating composition, it soon spread to the entire army.

[6] Following the February Revolution, the majority of political parties advocated remaining in the war, with the exception of the Bolsheviks, who had been staunchly opposed to it from the start. It is likely that these orators were Bolsheviks. There were many rumors that circulated in both Russian and Western societies that the Bolsheviks were German agents working to undermine the war effort.

and who contended that Austrian and German prisoners should be as well treated as Russian soldiers.[7]

In Petrograd food conditions were even worse than when I left. White bread could not be obtained at all and it was difficult to get sugar, jam being used in the best hotels to sweeten coffee or tea. Well-dressed individuals carried their own bread into the best cafes. A portion of the bread would be consumed at the meal and the remainder would be carefully wrapped up and taken away again.

The news of Kerensky's offensive[8] and its ultimate collapse reached me while crossing Siberia,[9] and I had expected to find the Petrograd populace gloomy and downcast by its failure.

As a matter of fact, however, things were going on just the same as ever. The cafes were crowded. The Nevsky[10] was thronged with the usual summer-night crowd, and nobody seemed to care much whether the army had been defeated or not. Shortly after my arrival in Petrograd, Rega[11] was evacuated, and while this caused a flurry of excitement for a day or so, the rumors of the counterrevolution inaugurated by General Korniloff[12] soon caused even this disaster to be forgotten. They were all so interested in what was happening in the interior that they paid little attention to the front.

---

[7] The treatment of Austrian and German prisoners of war was ostensibly regulated by the Red Cross, but their conditions were not very good. Indeed, Russian prisoners of war in Austria-Hungary and Germany were often treated better. For more, see the chapters on prisoners of war in Stoff, et al., *Military Experiences*.

[8] See note 3, page 5, on the Kerensky Offensive.

[9] This information does not seem to accord with that Grow provided in the Foreword, where he claimed to be at the front in July 1917, when the Kerensky Offensive was taking place, and observing the breakdown of discipline in the army firsthand.

[10] Nevsky Prospect, the main thoroughfare in Petrograd.

[11] Riga, the capital of Latvia. The evacuation occurred in August 1917. The Russian army left on September 2. The Germans entered the city on September 3.

[12] Known as the Kornilov Affair, this refers to an attempted military coup by General Lavr Kornilov against Kerensky's Provisional Government and the Petrograd Soviet of Soldiers' and Workers' Deputies (with which the Provisional Government was sharing power) in mid-August 1917. Kornilov had been the commander in chief of the Russian army and, in response to the unrest in Petrograd (known as the "July Days," when many came out into the streets to express dissatisfaction with the Provisional Government), believed it was necessary to bring troops to the capital to restore order, and, in particular, eliminate the Soviet and the influence of the Bolsheviks. There is some dispute as to whether Kornilov attempted to impose a military dictatorship or merely help shore up the Provisional Government, but the attempt was a failure and Kerensky perceived his actions as a threat, and therefore allied himself with the Soviet and armed it, including the Bolsheviks, to stop Kornilov. Kornilov's forces were defeated, he was removed from his post, arrested, and held in Bykhov Fortress. He managed to escape his imprisonment in the chaos created by the October Revolution, when the Bolsheviks seized power (November 7, NS) and raised an army to try to defeat them in the ensuing Civil

Things were happening fast and furious. Today a new Minister of Agriculture was appointed: tomorrow he was removed. An American I knew, who was attempting to do business with one of the departments, in the space of two weeks signed contracts with no less than six different Ministers!

There is no doubt that the soldiers were all very sincere in their support of the Revolution. They felt that it meant the salvation of Russia.

I met a number of officers I had known who had been discharged by their men![13] They had come back to Petrograd like lost sheep. They had absolutely nothing to do. Thousands of them, indeed, had enlisted as privates in the Death Battalions[14] and great numbers of them had been killed in the recent offensive.

When the prisons in Petrograd were opened after the Revolution, the Kerensky government made the mistake of sending great numbers of the prisoners to the front. Together with paid German propagandists they entered the ranks and bred discontent and confusion among the soldiers.

At Rega, I was told, men in German pay had cried out, during a German attack on a vital point, that the German cavalry had broken through and were in back of them—spreading panic among the poorly disciplined men and causing them to break and flee before the Germans.

An army commanded by the soldiers themselves was quite incapable of conducting any military movement. Strategy cannot be conducted from one point in the line. It must be directed by one who is far back of the front and can view the situation as whole.

The generals were powerless to maintain discipline. The soldiers' committees arrested them when they gave orders which did not suit the troops.

War. He died in the fighting in April 1918. See George Katkov, *Russia 1917, the Kornilov Affair: Kerensky and the Break-up of the Russian Army* (London: Longman, 1980).

[13] One of the results of the dissemination of Order No. 1 was that soldiers' committees sometimes voted to remove their officers.

[14] Death battalions were among a number of innovative military units created during 1917, beginning in the spring, in order to improve the failing morale of the army, in addition to other such units, such as "shock" formations. They were intended to serve as examples of extreme bravery, leading wavering soldiers into battle. While shock formations were organized as part of the regular army, death battalions were additional units to be attached to field divisions. They were mostly organized by volunteers in the rear and wore special insignia: black and red skull-and-crossbones. By the time of the October Revolution, there were over 300 such units, with 600,000 members. Among them were a number of all-female combat units, including the 1st Russian Women's Battalion of Death, the 2nd Moscow Women's Battalion of Death, and the 3rd Kuban Women's Shock Battalion, in which thousands of women enlisted. See Svetlana A. Solntseva, "The Russian Army's Shock Formations in 1917," *Russian Studies in History* 51, no. 4 (2013): 50–73, and Laurie S. Stoff, *They Fought for the Motherland: Russia's Women Soldiers in World War I and the Revolution* (Lawrence: University Press of Kansas, 2006).

Had the new government taken a firm stand from the beginning and refused to recognize the soldiers' committees, backing up the generals and officers in their efforts to enforce discipline, retaining the death penalty for insubordination, the Russian army would remain today an important factor in the war.[15]

It was an appalling fact that this magnificent fighting machine, composed of twelve million soldiers, who, at the time I was with them, had been as fine fighting men as the world had ever seen, could now be absolutely inert without ever having been seriously defeated in the field.

At no time since the beginning of the war had the Germans killed, wounded, or captured sufficient numbers of the Russian soldiers or taken sufficient material to destroy them as an active offensive agent. The paralysis of this huge army had been accomplished without the loss of a man by the insidious but wonderfully effective agencies of intrigue and propaganda.[16]

---

[15] Like Grow, many officers and conservatives believed that the transfer of power from officers to soldiers through Order No. 1 was the undoing of the Russian army. This belies the fact that decomposition was already an established fact long before the order was issued, and in fact, in a number of ways, the order actually worked to at least temporarily stabilize the situation and allow the soldiers to continue fighting, albeit purely to defend against further enemy advances in order to protect the revolution. Ultimately, however, the order could not stem the unraveling of the army, which continued to deteriorate as soldiers became increasingly unwilling to go on the attack and desperately wanted to return home. See Wildman, *The Road to Soviet Power and Peace*, and Sanborn, *Imperial Apocalypse*.

[16] Strange and largely inaccurate commentary, considering the numerous defeats that the Russian army had suffered in battles from the very beginning of the war and the continued problems it faced. By 1917, it had lost half of its troops (7.5 million of a force of 15 million) and vast amounts of territory. The Kerensky Offensive, as Grow admitted above, was a failure. The Germans had captured Riga and were encroaching on Petrograd.

Chapter XXV
AFTER THE REVOLUTION

Col. Kalpaschnecoff was in Petrograd, where he occupied an important position in the newly organized Red Cross. He was trying in every possible way to help this organization, which had been badly handicapped by the removal of many of the officers and by the difficulty in getting men to carry on their work conscientiously. Not only had this excess of liberty spread among the soldiers but also among the orderlies in the army and the workmen in the factories.

The Twenty-first Flying Column was temporarily commanded during the Colonel's absence by another man.

I desired to return to the front and visit my old corps, so that I could see for myself the conditions existing in the army, and the Colonel quickly secured permission for me to do so.

One day in August we accordingly set forth in a second-class coach from the Nicholas Station on a train bound for the front.

"General Pleschcoff left the corps a month ago and returned to his home near Vladivostock," said the Colonel, as we closed the door of our compartment and settled back in our seats, preparing for the long ride ahead of us. "He found he could no longer have any discipline in the corps, so he gave it up. You remember General Padgoursky,[1] who commanded the First Division—the very fat one with the red face? He too was discharged by the soldiers but he re-enlisted as a private. He lived in the trenches with them, ate the same food, and slept in the same dug-outs—the men whom he had formerly commanded. When the attack in July occurred, he was the first man over the top, and although sixty-six years of age he led his men into the first-line trenches where he bayonetted two Germans, and then he started on alone for the German second-line. The Germans had concentrated a great many machine-guns and men in their second-line, and they turned a terrific fire on him as he dashed

---

[1] Fedor A. Podgursky (1860–1929), a nobleman from Nizhny Novgorod. He graduated from the Constantine Military Academy and was commissioned an ensign in the Russian Imperial Army. He had risen to the rank of lieutenant general by the time the war broke out. In 1915, he was given command of the First Siberian Division, a post he held until July 1917, during which time his unit participated in the Lake Naroch Offensive. Following the Bolshevik Revolution, he voluntarily joined the Red Army in 1918 and served on its General Staff. There is no record of his enlistment as a private, but he was awarded a St. George's Cross in November 1917.

across the intervening space. He was wounded twice but kept going, and his men, seeing their old commander all alone and about to plunge into a trench full of Germans, followed him—and they took the second German line! During the hand-to-hand fighting he was bayonetted through the shoulder. They held the second-line until the battalion on their right gave way in the face of a German counter-attack and they were forced to retire, carrying back the wounded ex-general, who raved and cursed all the way to the Russian trenches. Then the men decided they wanted him back as commander, so they discharged the general who was commanding the division and gave him back his old place. We shall probably see him on our arrival."

This General Padgoursky had always had the reputation of being a fire-eater and was known to be a very brave man. He had been wounded four times in the Japanese war, twice before in the present war and now, with his three additional wounds, had a grand total of nine wounds.

In the corridor of the car we met an old acquaintance—a man who had been a colonel in the old days. He now had the uniform of an under officer with the red and black ribbon of the Death Battalion on his arm.

"Things are frightful at the front," he said. "I was removed from my command and I enlisted in one of the Death Battalions. I have lost all my property. The peasants confiscated it. My house was looted and burned and I am almost penniless.[2] The soldiers at the front stole all my equipment and I have just been to Petrograd to buy a new one."

The next day we found the cars packed to suffocation with soldiers who were apparently riding about merely for the novelty of the experience. Where they were going or for what reason, God only knows. They surely did not seem to have any objective. They crowded into the first and second class cars and stood stolidly in the corridors jamming the compartments. When the conductor asked for their place-cards, they replied: "Tickets! We have no tickets! Isn't Russia free? Can't we ride where we wish without paying?" The poor train official would wildly expostulate but, unable to pierce their armor of childlike blandness, would disappear waving his hands hopelessly in the air.

After three days we reached the little station near the front, where we were met by our old battered victoria driven by one of the orderlies who had worked with us through so many months of active fighting.

The drive to the base of our old column was about fifteen miles. Although it was in August when they should be at their best, the roads were almost impassable because for over six months the soldiers had absolutely refused to do a bit of road mending or road-making. They were worn and torn by the innumerable wheels of

---

[2] During the summer of 1917, there was a great deal of unrest in the Russian countryside, as many peasants, frustrated with the lack of action on the part of the Provisional Government to redistribute land, attacked landlords and looted their homes.

transport and artillery until they had holes in them which were big enough almost to swallow a horse and wagon.

We passed many groups of soldiers lolling in the fields along the roadsides or strolling about smoking the inevitable pungent *makorka* and orating. They didn't salute us as we passed.

We finally arrived at the base of the column, where I was effusively greeted by the tall lean student Nicholi, the new doctor and Michael, my old orderly. Michael begged me to take him back with me to Petrograd, explaining that it was impossible for him to do any work under the rule of the committees. I said I would try to get him into the Red Cross.

They told me that in the July offensive they had had the greatest difficulty to make the men work more than eight hours a day because some of the larger committees, who correspond with the I. W. W.[3] of America, had told them that if they worked more than eight hours they would be hurting the Revolution, and the poor ignorant overgrown children implicitly believed all they were told.

In the afternoon we went to the staff of the First Siberian Army Corps. It was located in what had formerly been the beautiful country house of some wealthy landowner but it was now dilapidated and dirty. There were no sentries on guard, and a crowd of ill-kept soldiers was lounging about in the reception-room. No one paid the slightest attention to us, and it was only with great difficulty that the Colonel abstracted one of the individuals from some engrossing conversation which they were carrying on and asked him to call the officer of the day.

He slouched off, without saluting, and returned presently with a man who had evidently been recently promoted, for he was neither courteous nor showed any of the signs of culture and breeding which marked the officers of the old army. We asked to see the commander of the corps and were ushered into the "operation room" of the staff where all the orders are issued; and there we met the little mouse-like individual who was in command. He was pleasant and courteous enough, but one could see at a glance that he was the type of man who would be absolutely under the thumb of the soldiers' committees. As long as he retained sufficient meekness of spirit his position and his neck would probably be safe.

We secured permission to visit the trenches, and the next morning rode out to the first division on horseback. Things were in better shape there than at any other point we had so far visited. This was brave General Padgoursky's division. As we approached the staff we saw this huge corpulent man seated under an apple-tree by a table, drinking tea. In front of the house stood two sentries who presented arms as we passed. It looked more like the army of the old days and it was a relief to see a bit of discipline after the weeks of chaos through which I had passed.

---

[3] Industrial Workers of the World, international labor union with ties to socialist labor movement.

The old General was swathed in bandages which made his rotund figure more bulky than ever and his arm was carried in a sling, but he arose and waddled toward us his red face beaming, and breathing noisily as he came. We talked over old times, and as we were leaving he remarked: "It is all right just now, but who can tell when they will turn on me like a pack of wolves because I insist on discipline, and then—*finis* Padgoursky. *Nu nichevo!* (Well, it is nothing.)"

In the trenches of the first division discipline was on a fairly high plane but things were very quiet. The men sat about in their dug-outs and in the trenches smoking and singing and playing the balalika[4] and but for the fact that they did not expose themselves above the trench parapets one would have thought the enemy was a thousand miles away.

Sanitary conditions were very bad in the trenches and we were told that great numbers of the men were ill with scurvy because of the poor food.

In the second division we found the discipline of a very low order and we went away heartsick at the deterioration of our old First Siberian Corps—the Ironside Corps of the Russian Army. I spent a week at the front, visiting different regiments; and while conditions varied, one could see that unless some very radical change were made, the Russian army as an active offensive agent was a thing of the past.

On my return to Petrograd I found the city highly excited at the report of the advance of Korniloff in his effort to wrest the reins of government from Kerensky and establish a dictatorship—which we all thought would be about the best thing that could happen;[5] but this hope flickered out with the failure of the Korniloff movement and we could see that things were rapidly drifting from bad to worse.

I left Russia before the Bolsheviki[6] party overthrew the Kerensky government and took control of the affairs of Russia.

It is with sadness that I read of the further disintegration and demoralization of the Russian fighting machine, and yet I cannot but feel that it did a lot for us when it was in its prime. It was by the Russians' great sacrifices early in the war, when the Germans were sweeping across the fields of France and the fate of Paris—of France—yes, I may say of the whole world—hung trembling in the balance, that the tide of the onrushing Teuton flood was stemmed by the Russian advances into Austria and East Prussia.

Again, during that bloody fighting on the western front near Lake ———, in which I participated and in which our losses were so frightful, there is no doubt that the Russians did much to relieve the pressure on the French at Verdun.

---

[4] *Balalaika*, a triangular stringed instrument with a hollow body and three strings that are plucked, like a guitar, usually to play traditional Russian folk music.

[5] Interesting that despite his earlier comments about wanting the new democracy to succeed, Grow now advocated for military dictatorship.

[6] The Bolshevik Revolution occurred on November 7 (NS), 1917.

Then Brusiloff, in his great drive in the summer of 1916—during which he captured 400,000 prisoners in three months—relieved the hard-pressed Italians and forced twenty-two divisions of Austro-Germans who were concentrated on their narrow front and who were pouring through the Alpine pass to be withdrawn and sent to the north to check the Russian onslaught. The Russians undoubtedly saved the Italians at that time from the disaster which subsequently overcame them after the Russians had been eliminated as a factor in the war.

Yes, I think the Russians have done their bit. I recall the hundreds of thousands of lonely graves scattered over the barren fields and the dark forest and the gloomy swamps of Poland and Galicia and I know that these brave Russian lads did not die in vain.

INDEX

Alexander II, Tsar, viii
American, vii–ix, xiii, xvii, xviii, xx, 7, 9, 12, 15, 17, 20, 23, 25, 33, 41, 48, 56, 64, 67, 98, 132, 141
Aero Medical Laboratory, ix
African, xiv, 130
Arapoff, Gregory Paulovitch, 111
Archangel, 99
Austrians, 100, 102, 109–117, 123, 128, 132, 133, 139, 140
Austro-Germans, 118, 119, 128, 147
Astoria Hotel, 11, 12, 23, 24

balalika (*balalaika*), 146
Boches, 42, 49, 55, 57, 61, 81, 101
bonyah, 64
Belorussia, x
Benz limosine, 65, 66
blockie, 51
Bolsheviks (Bolsheviki), xx, 146
Brusiloff, 100, 102, 109, 133, 147
Bukhovina, x

Camac, John Burgess, viii
Carpathians, 100
Caucasus, 31
Caviar, 12
Ceslivano Station, 30, 65
Christiana, ix, 138
Commander of the Corps, 34, 35, 145
Coney Island, 105
Cossack, 12, 38, 65, 66, 75, 127, 131, 132
Cross of St. George, xiii
Czar, 12, 18, 63, 66

deenshick, 30
Droshky, 11, 18
Dumbrofsky, Captain, 13
Dvinsk, 11

Egbert, Dr. Edward, vii, xii, 9, 11–16, 24–26, 54
Eitel Friederich, Prince, 66
English, xiv, xv, 6, 7, 13, 15, 19, 23, 33, 35, 39, 43, 36, 48, 50, 64, 67, 132, 138
Entente, xiv, xxi
Europe, 9, 11, 24

Farnum biplane, 134
February Revolution, ix, xvii, xix–xxi
Finland, 21, 99
First (1st) Siberian Army Corps, viii, xvi, 22, 27, 35, 66, 97, 145
First World War (World War I), vii
French, 7, 12, 96, 146
Frost King, 97
Flying Column, 21st, viii, 22, 23

Galicia, x, 10, 35, 100, 147
Galoopchick, 46, 73, 90
Geneva Convention, xiii
Germans, viii, x, xiv, 5, 6, 34, 38, 41, 42, 44, 46, 47, 53, 58–61, 66, 71, 73–78, 81, 83, 87, 89, 90, 96, 100, 102, 104–06, 109, 114, 118–21, 124, 128–32, 136, 140–44, 146, 147
Grow, Malcom Cummings, vii–xxi, 11, 17, 31, 98
Gulf of Finland, 14

Holy Russia, 78
Hotel Willard, 9
Howitzer, 55, 84, 115
Hussar Hospital, vii, 12, 17, 18, 20, 23

Industrial Workers of the World (IWW), xx, 145
Ironside Corps, 22, 146
isba, 111
isvoscheek, 15, 16, 25

Italians, 100, 134, 147

Jefferson Medical College, vii
Joselyn, 79

Kaiser, 66
Kalpaschnecoff (Kalpanshnikov-Camac, Colonel Andrei Ivanovich), vii, viii, xvi, 22, 23, 25, 26, 27, 31, 35, 36, 38, 39, 42, 45–48, 63, 67, 68, 95, 97, 98, 101, 102, 108–110, 114–117, 138, 143, 145
Kennan, George, xviii, xx
Kolky, 116
Kovel, 109
Kamerad, 60
Kerensky, Alexander, 5, 141, 146
Kiev, vii, 9, 10, 24
kinjal, 43
Kirkwall, 138
Kornilov (Koriloff), xx, 146
Kronstadt, 14

Legion of Merit, ix
Lenin, Vladimir, xx
Lithuania, x
Lodz, 35

Maria Alexandrovna, Baroness, 18, 21
Masurian Lakes, x
Medal (Cross of) of St. George, 28, 34, 97–99, 143
Metia (Mitia), 33, 34, 36–38, 40, 41, 44, 45, 50, 84, 105, 124, 127, 128, 135, 136
Mogheliv, 18
makorka, 31, 56, 145
Mendelssohn, 41
Minister of Agriculture, 141
Ministers of War and Munitions, 44
Muhanoff, Lieutenant, 47, 48, 50, 53–55, 60, 62, 75, 82, 83, 91, 103, 106, 119, 122

Nemets, 13, 79, 89
Nevsky, 16, 140
New York, xvi, 11, 48
Nicholas, Grand Duke, 19, 35, 68
Nicholas II, Tsar, vii
Nicholi Alexandrovitch, 45, 60, 61
Nicholiavsky Station, 26

No Man's Land, 39, 46, 48, 50, 56, 57, 59, 60, 70–73, 81, 82, 86, 87, 96, 109, 119, 123–25
Norway, 99

October Revolution, ix
Olga Michaelovna, 18, 19
Omsk, 43
Outlook, The, xviii
Order of St. Stanislaus, xiii

Padgoursky, General, 143–46
Paris, viii, 146
Pennsylvania, 129
Penza, vii
Peter the Great, Tsar, viii
Petrograd, vii–xii, xvi, xxi, 11, 13, 17, 18, 20, 24, 25, 28, 44, 64, 68, 76, 96, 98, 99, 100, 137–46
Philadelphia, vii, viii, xii, 9
Pleschcoff, General, 3, 43, 65–68, 75, 97, 143
Poland, x, 147
Postovy, xvi, 80
Prosnitch, 35
Provisional Government, xvi, xviii, xx
Prussian, 7, 109

Rasputin, 137
Red Cross, vii–xiv, 9, 23, 24, 114, 118, 130, 139, 143, 145
Rega (Riga), 141
River Stockhod, 109, 115
River Styr, 116, 117
Rodzianko, Mikhail, xiii
rooboshka (ruboshka), 78, 106, 113
Rovno, 109, 114, 133
Rubinstein, 41
Russian Civil War, xxi
Russian Duma, xiii
Russian Embassy, viii, 23
Russian Imperial Army, viii, x, xi
Russian Imperial Army Medical Corps, viii
Russian Women's Battalion of Death, xvi
Russo-Japanese War, x

Saint George, Medal of (Cross of), 28, 34, 97, 98
sanitar, 59
Saparoff, Lieutenant, 122

Saratoff, 33
Siberians, 35, 64, 83, 118, 126, 137
Smolensk, 82
Swedish, 132

Tannenburg, x
Tartar, 13
Tatiana Alexandrovna, Princess, 20
Teuton, 146
Tolstoy, Lev, 102
Trans-Siberian Railroad, 43
Trotsky, Lev, xx
Tsarskoe Selo, vii, xv, xvi, 17–23

Union of Towns, xi
Union of Zemstvos, xi
US Army Medical Service, ix

Verdun, 96, 146
verst, 64, 98, 102
Vicker, Dr., 17, 19–22
Vilna, 75
Vladivostok (Vladivostock), ix, 139, 143

Warsaw, xiii, 34, 35, 109
Washington, DC, vii, viii, 9, 23
Wright-Patterson Air Force Base, ix

zachowsky, 12, 27
zemlanka, 38

www.ingramcontent.com/pod-product-compliance
Lightning Source LLC
Chambersburg PA
CBHW032026230426
43671CB00005B/217